OFFICIAL'S MANUAL:
VOLLEYBALL

OFFICIAL'S MANUAL:

VOLLEYBALL

2nd Edition

James A. Peterson, Ph.D.
Women's Sports Foundation

Robert A. Bertucci
University of Tennessee

Leisure Press
P.O. Box 3
West Point, N.Y. 10996

A publication of Leisure Press.
P.O. Box 3, West Point, N.Y. 10996
Copyright©1979, 1982 Leisure Press
All rights reserved. Printed in the U.S.A.

ISBN 0-88011-078-3
Library of Congress Number 82-81450

Illustrations by Carol A. Johnson

Contents

1
The Game

The game of volleyball, the leading competitive sport in 25 countries today, is actually of American origin. It was invented in 1895 by William G. Morgan, physical education director of the Holyoke, Massachusetts, YMCA. There were some who said the game was of Italian origin which had traveled to Germany. However, Morgan vigorously defended the originality of his ideas.

The new game was developed in an attempt to fill a need for businessmen of the Holyoke area who wished to workout daily but who were unable to participate in as strenuous a game as basketball. Gradually the game of volleyball evolved. The original ball used was a basketball. This soon proved to be too heavy and the Spalding Company was asked to make one of soft calfskin. The net was set up at 6 feet 6 inches and the team consisted of 5 players each.

Orinally, there were no hard and fast rules. However, as the game became better known, rules began to evolve. In 1897 the first of them was printed in the Handbook of the Athletic League of the Young Men's Christian Association of North America. It was this Handbook which YMCA directors carried with them to all parts of the world and which served to popularize the game for all time. Nevertheless, play was still a rather haphazard affair. The numbers of players depended upon the number of participants present; the size of the court depended upon the room available, and so on.

Eventually, the rules and regulations began to go through periods of change. The height of the net was raised to 7 feet 6 inches; the rule concerning dribbling was eliminated; and 21 points was established as the winning score. In 1920 the size of the court and composition of the ball were standardized. Still, the basic game remained the same.

Volleyball gained further popularity during World War I. Again, the YMCA under the leadership of George J. Fisher, used the game to increase the level of physical fitness of the participants, this time for the troops. It was a case of mass participation with once again no set rules but tremendous enthusiasm.

By 1924 the game began to appear on college campuses. Slowly scholastic volleyball programs were instituted, varsity teams organized and awards presented. Colleges began scheduling matches with each other, and by 1946 clubs were being organized.

Volleyball was invented in 1895 by an American — William G. Morgan.

The United States Volleyball Association was formed in 1928 with the primary purpose of coordinating volleyball rules and the creation of a National Open Tournament. Its first president was Dr. George J. Fisher, the same Dr.Fisher who so ably helped introduce volleyball to the Allied troops during World War I. The USVBA is now made up of at least 22 different organizations including the National Council of YMCA's. It publishes annually a rule book. It organizes a national tournament in several divisions to include the collegiate division, the women's open division, the YMCA division, the senior men's division and the men's open division. In spite of all these activities and more, the only paid official is the Executive Secretary and this action was taken as late as 1975. Otherwise, everyone involved from the officials who officiate at local games, the sponsoring organizations, to teachers of physical education — all donate their services to the cause of good sportsmanship and fair play.

Of course, it is impossible to determine the number of people who play the game of volleyball worldwide today, some estimates range as high as 80 million participants, but it is known that as a highly competitive sport, it is one of the most popular games in the world. The admission of the game to the official list of sports in the Olympic Games in 1964 was the only step in awarding Volleyball the recognition it so richly deserves. Volleyball is here to stay.

2
Prerequisites of Good Officiating

A well-officiated volleyball game is a common goal of coaches, players, fans, and officials alike. However, in order to reach the level of officiating desired, volleyball officials must possess certain basic prerequisites:

- **Knowledge of rules.** Knowledge of the rules is absolutely essential for quality officiating. Maintaining this knowledge is equally important. Some umpires mistakenly assume that once certification from a local officials' association is obtained, their exposure to the rules has ended. Good officials not only review the rules before each season but also refer to special situations before and after each game. Rule changes in the game of volleyball occur each year; it is the responsibility of every volleyball official to keep abreast of these changes. The game of volleyball is complicated and is constantly undergoing revision. New interpretations and points of emphasis are presented with each year's new USVBA rule book.

  Knowledge of the rules as written in the rule book is obviously desirable; however, proper application of this knowledge to the game situation is essential to good officiating. The rules were written to insure fair play. The proper application and enforcement of the rules should be the foremost goal of all good officials.

- **Good judgment.** Because many of the "calls" made by a volleyball offical are "judgment calls", proper judgment is a very important ingredient in the make-up of a good official. Some individuals claim that judgment cannot be taught. They feel it is an inherited quality; the individual either has it or he doesn't. This is not completely true. Good judgment is the ability to see a situation and to make the correct response to that situation. Good judgment is made up of three parts: perception, position and experience. Perception is the ability to

Good judgment is the ability to see a situation and to make the correct response to that situation.

look at a situation and ascertain what is truly taking place. It is the ability to block out competing visual and audio stimuli and to devote complete attention to the situation at hand. True perception is not possible from an improper position. An official with the best judgment in the world cannot exercise his judgment unless he is in the correct position to insure true perception. When perception is learned and proper position insured, experience becomes the best teacher of good judgment. The ability to concentrate on specific areas where rule violations occur is a continuing process for the good official. The ability to look past the extraneous action and to pinpoint the position of the ball or the placement of a player's hands, for example, is enhanced every time that particular situation is presented to the official. Identical to the learning of any skill, the presentation of a situation and the eliciting of the correct response increase the likelihood of that same response being elicited the next time that situation is encountered.

- **Consistency.** Managers and players often mention inconsistency as the most upsetting quality an official can possess. Consistent interpretation and administration of the rules are probably the most important qualities an umpire can demonstrate. True consistency does not mean attempting to equalize the rule interpretations for both teams, but rather interpreting each situation as a distinct, separate part of the game. The previous call, or the next call to be made, should not have any influence upon the situation under consideration. Consistency means calling a repeated play late in the match the same way you called it on the first serve.

- **Decisiveness.** Volleyball officiating requires instantaneous, judgmental decisions. In order to minimize the amount of controversy generated by these decisions, they should be made with the greatest degree of decisiveness possible. Each decision is always open to the "rose colored" interpretation of the players, managers, coaches and fans; therefore, the good official will "sell" his call to the game participants. This selling process should start with the *immediate* execution of the proper hand signal.

  Controversial calls are always subject to criticism. However, the call that is made decisively minimizes the controversy. These decisions should be made in a way that will leave no question in the minds of players, coaches, or fans as to the correctness of that decision. In general, the more potential for question, the greater the degree of decisiveness required.

- **Confidence.** Confidence and decisiveness are closely related. Confidence deals more with the attitude of the official and the impression he makes on fans, players, and coaches while decisiveness is concentrated on the mechanics of officiating. Anxiety and self-doubt have no place in the mind of the

Volleyball officiating requires instantaneous, judgmental decisions.

good official. When mentally preparing to work a volleyball match, an official must be absolutely confident of his ability to maintain control of the game.

Confidence is gained through experience and knowledge of the game. The confident official should be aware of all the possible situations that can arise and should be prepared with the correct response. Confidence is reflected in the attitude, voice projection and game control of every good official.

- **Fairness.** Some call it honesty and some call it integrity, but uppermost in the mind of all officials should be a personal commitment to fairness. The intent of the official is to equally apply a set of pre-designated rules to both teams so that neither team is placed at a disadvantage. This can only be accomplished through complete fairness. Fairness has many enemies. The good official must be aware of all the possible areas in which fairness can be compromised. Coaches, players and spectators alike frequently intimidate an official through verbal abuse and crowd-inciting gestures. The good official should either control this action through application of "game-conduct" decorum rules or completely ignore these attempts at influence. In every instance, an official should objectively view each situation independent of the effect on the crowd, players or game.

- **Courage.** In order to implement all those qualities required of the good official, he must possess a great deal of courage. Officials are often referred to in the same breath as the opponent and generally are not liked by either team. This is most unfortunate because they are as necessary to the game as either team, both coaches, and all the fans. Courageous officials must make decisions without regard for the score, its effect on the players, fans, coaches, or game, and independent from all the pressures applied both internally and externally. The courageous official must place fairness above all else and strive to "call them as he sees them." The ability to resist pressure and intimidation determine the reputation of the official. Honest, fair officiating is appreciated by everyone involved in the game.

3
OFFICIAL 1982 – 1984 UNITED STATES VOLLEYBALL RULES

as approved by
The United States Volleyball Association

The United States Volleyball Rules are those of the International Volleyball Federation as adopted by the United States Volleyball Association, the National Governing Body for Volleyball in the United States. The IVBF rules are used world wide. It is difficult to translate and interpret precisely these rules from one language to another. The United States rules shall be in effect through the conclusion of the 1984 Olympiad.

CHAPTER I
FACILITIES, PLAYING AREA AND EQUIPMENT

RULE 1. PLAYING AREA AND MARKINGS

Article 1. COURT—The playing court shall be 18 m. long by 9 m. wide (59' x 29'6"). A clear area of 2 m. (6'6") should surround an indoor court. A clear area of 3 m. (9'10") should surround an outdoor court.

Article 2. COURT MARKINGS — The court shall be marked by lines 5 cm. (2") wide. Areas being defined by court markings shall be measured from the outside edge of the lines defining such areas.

Article 3. CENTER LINE — A line 5 cm. (2") wide shall be drawn across the court beneath the net from side line to side line dividing the court into two equal team areas.

Article 4. ATTACK LINE — In each team area a line 5 cm. (2") wide shall be drawn between the side lines parallel to the center line and 3 m. (9'10") from the middle of the center line to the rearmost edge of the attack line. The attack area, limited by the center line and the attack line, extends indefinitely beyond the side lines.

Article 5. SERVICE AREA — At a point 20 cm. (8") behind and perpendicular to each end line, two lines, each 15 cm. (6") in length and 5 cm. (2") in width, shall be drawn to mark the service area for each team. One line is an extension of the right side line and the other is drawn so that its farther edge is 3 m. (9'10") from the extension of the outside edge of the right side line. The service area shall have a minimum depth of 2 m. (6'6").

Article 6. OVERHEAD CLEARANCE — For the Olympic Games there must be a clear space of 12 m. 50 cm. (41') above the court. For the final rounds of the World Championships, or similar competitions, the same clearance is required unless the Executive Committee of the International Volleyball Federation makes a special concession. For all other competition, there should be an overhead clearance free from obstructions to a height of 7 m. (23') measured from the playing surface.

Article 7. SUBSTITUTION ZONE — The substitution zone is an area extending from the imaginary extension of the attack line to the imaginary extension of the center line between the court boundary and the scorer's table.

Article 8. MINIMUM TEMPERATURE — The minimum temperature shall not be below 10 degrees centigrade (50 degrees farenheit).

COMMENTARY ON RULE 1
PLAYING FACILITIES

1) *COURT CLEARANCE — In order to provide adequate room for playing of the game, a clear space of 3 m. (9'10") should surround an outdoor court and a clear space of 2 m. (6'6") should surround an indoor court. For the Olympic Games, there should be a clearance behind the end lines of 8 m. (26') and beyond the side lines of 5 m. (16'6"). For the final rounds of the World Championships, and similar competitions, the same clearances are required unless the Executive Committee of the IVBF makes a special concession. The referees' stand must present the least possible obstacle. If the stand should present an unfair hindrance to play, or if low hanging objects protrude into the clear space specified above, the referee may direct a play-over if they interfere with play.*

2) *OTHER FACTORS — The court must be flat and horizontal. For outdoor courts a slope of 5 mm. per m. is allowable for drainage. The game may be played indoors or outdoors.*

3) *ASSUMED EXTENSION OF LINES — All lines on the court are considered to have an assumed indefinite extension.*

4) *CEILING CLEARANCE — For other than Olympic Games or World Championships, a ball contacting a ceiling or object connected to the ceiling shall remain in play if*

the ceiling is less than 7 m. above the playing surface. The ball may not legally strike above the opponent's area nor may it legally fall to the opponent's area after striking the ceiling or objects connected to the ceiling. Walls, or objects connected to walls, shall not be in play. Low objects protruding into the 2 m. free zone around the court may be ruled a play-over if they interfere with a play that could normally be made if the objects were not within the free zone.

5) UNSUITABLE COURTS—The court must be approved by the Special Referees Commission to be acceptable for competition in International matches. The court, in all cases, must be under the control of the first referee before a match. The first referee alone is responsible for deciding whether or not the court is suitable for play. The first referee will declare the court unfit for play in the following cases:
   a) If snow or rain has made the court soft or slippery.
   b) When play can be dangerous due to any hazardous condition of the court surface or equipment.
   c) When fog or darkness makes it impossible to officiate properly.

6) BAD WEATHER—In case of bad weather (thunderstorms, showers, high winds, etc.) the first referee can postpone the match or interrupt it.

7) BOUNDARY MARKERS—Wood, metal, or other solid material may not be used for outdoor courts since the ground can erode, thus causing lines to protrude above ground level and present a hazard to players. This applies to brick or other hard material. Hollowed out lines are not recommended. The court lines should be marked before the beginning of a match. On an outdoor court, the lines must be clearly marked with whitewash, chalk, or other substance which is not injurious to eyes or skin. No lime nor caustic material of any kind may be used. Lines must be marked in such a manner as to not make the ground uneven. Indoors the lines must be of a color contrasting to that of the floor. Light colors (white or yellow) are the most visible and are recommended.

8) LIGHTING—Lighting in a playing facility should be 500 to 1500 luxes measured at a point 1 m. above the playing surface.

9) SCOREBOARD—No special recommendations are made as to the size rf the scoreboard. It should be divided into two parts with large numbers to provide a running score for each team. The name or initials of the two teams should be shown at the top of each side. Information displayed on the scoreboard is not official and may not be used as a basis of protest.

10) ADJOINING COURTS—Where competition (including warmups preceding a match) is being conducted on adjoining courts, no player may penetrate into an adjoining court before, during or after playing the ball.

11) DIVIDING NETS OR OTHER PARTITIONS—Where dividing nets or other hanging partitions of a movable nature separate adjoining courts, only the player actually making the attempt to play the ball may go into the net or move it. It should be ruled a dead ball and a fault if a teammate, substitute, coach or other person deliberately moves the net to assist play.

12) BLEACHERS AND WALLS—Players may not enter bleachers for the purpose of playing the ball. Players making a play on the ball over bleachers must have a foot in contact with the floor if the remaining foot is contacting a bleacher at the time of contact with the ball. After contact with the ball, players may enter the

bleachers without penalty. When playing the ball near a wall, players may not use the wall to gain a height advantage. If the wall is contacted by the foot of a player prior to making contact of the ball, at least one foot must be on the floor at the time the ball is contacted.

RULE 2. THE NET

Article 1. SIZE AND CONSTRUCTION — The net shall be not less than 9.50 m. (32') in length and 1 m. (39") in width throughout the full length when stretched. A double thickness of white canvas 5 cm. (2") wide shall be sewn along the full length of the top of the net. A flexible wire rope shall be stretched through the upper canvas and the lower edge of the net. The end of the net shall be capable of receiving a wooden dowel to keep the ends of the net in straight lines when tight. For detailed specifications, see the section on specifications approved by the USVBA Equipment Committee.

Article 2. NET HEIGHT — The height of the net measured from the center of the court shall be 2.43 m. (7'11 5/8") for men and 2.24 m. (7'4 1/8") for women. The two ends of the net must be at the same height from the playing surface and cannot exceed the regulation height by more than 2 cm. (3/4").

Article 3. VERTICAL TAPE MARKERS — Two tapes of white material 5 cm. (2") wide and 1 m. (39") in length shall be fastened to the net, one at each end, over and perpendicular to each side line and the center line. The vertical tape side markers are considered to be a part of the net.

Article 4. NET ANTENNAS — Coinciding with the outside edge of each vertical tape marker, an antenna shall be fastened to the net at a distance of 9 m. (29'6") from each other. The net antennas shall be 1.80 m. (6') in length and made of safe and moderately flexible material with a uniform diameter of 10 mm. (3/8"). The upper half of each antenna shall be marked with alternating white and red or orange bands not less than 10 cm. (4") and not more than 15 cm. (6") in width. The antennas will be affixed to the net with fasteners that provide for quick and easy adjustment of the antenna. The fasteners shall be smooth surfaced and free of any sharp edges that might be considered hazardous to players.

Article 5. NET SUPPORTS — Where possible, the posts, uprights, or stands, including their bases, which support the net should be at least 50 cm. (19 1/2") from the side lines and placed in such a manner as to not interfere with the officials in the performance of their duties.

COMMENTARY ON RULE 2
THE NET

1) NET SUPPORTS — Round net support posts are preferable since they are convenient for the referees and are less hazardous to the players. They must be of a length that allows the net to be fixed at the correct height above the playing surface. Fixing the posts to the floor by means of wire supports should be avoided if possible. If wire supports are necessary, they should be covered with a soft material to provide protection for the players. It is recommended that strips of material be hung from the wire to alert players of their presence.

2) *NET ADJUSTMENTS — The height and tension of the net must be measured before the start of the match and at any other time the first referee deems advisable. Height measurements should be made in the center of the court and at each end of the net perpendicular to the side boundary lines to assure that each end of the net is within the prescribed variation. The net must be tight throughout its length. After being tightened, the net should be checked to assure that a ball striking the net will rebound properly.*

3) *ANTENNAS AND VERTICAL MARKERS — Antennas and vertical tape markers on the net should be checked by the first referee before a match to assure that they are properly located on the net, are properly secured and properly aligned. Special attention should be given to any exposed ends at the bottom of the antennas to assure that they are smooth and round or are covered with tape so as not to present a safety hazard to players.*

4) *NET TORN DURING PLAY — If a net becomes torn during play, other than a served ball contacting the net, play shall be stopped and a play-over directed after the net is repaired or replaced.*

CURRENT PRACTICES FOR RULE 2

1) NET HEIGHTS FOR AGE GROUPS — The following net heights are currently in practice for the below indicated age groups:

HEIGHT OF NET

AGE GROUPS	GIRLS	BOYS
11 years and under	1.85 m. (6'1")	1.85 m. (6'1")
13 years and under	2.12 m. (7'2 1/16")	2.24 m. (7'4 1/8")
16 years and under	2.24 m. (7'4 1/8")	2.43 m. (7'11 5/8")
19 years and under	2.24 m. (7'4 1/8")	2.43 m. (7'11 5/8")

RULE 3. THE BALL

Article 1. SIZE AND CONSTRUCTION — The ball shall be spherical with a laceless leather or leatherlike cover of 12 or more pieces of uniform light color with or without a separate bladder; it shall not be less than 62 cm. nor more than 68 cm. (25" to 27") in circumference; and it shall weigh not less than 260 grams nor more than 280 grams (9 to 10 oz.) See detailed specification approved by the USVBA Committee on Equipment.

COMMENTARY ON RULE 3
THE BALL

1) *APPROVAL OF BALLS — Balls used for any international match must be those approved by IVBF. Balls used for sanctioned USVBA competitions must be those approved by the USVBA Committee on Equipment.*

2) *RESPONSIBILITY FOR EXAMINING BALL PRIOR TO PLAY — It is the responsibility of the first referee to examine the balls prior to the start of a match to determine that they are official and in proper condition. A ball that becomes wet or slippery*

during competition must be changed.

3) *PRESSURE OF THE BALL*—*The pressure of the ball, measured with a special pressure gauge, must be between 0.40 and 0.45 kg/cm^2 (5.5 to 6.5 lbs/sq. in.). However, the structure of the ball may affect the maximum variation of the pressure allowed; for this reason, jurys of international competition may reduce this margin of difference within the above range.*

4) *MARKINGS ON THE BALLS*—*A maximum of 25% of the total exterior surface area of the ball may be covered with logo, name, identification and other markings and coloring, which is to say that a minimum of 75% of the exterior surface of an approved ball shall be of uniform light color.*

5) *THREE BALL SYSTEM DURING A MATCH*—*The following procedures will be followed when using the three ball systems during a match:*

   a) *Six (6) ball retrievers will be used and shall be stationed as follows: (1) One at each corner of the court about 8 m. from the end lines and 4 m. to 5 m. from the side lines; (2) One behind the scorer; (3) One behind the referee. (NOTE: Ball retrievers may use chairs)*

   b) *At the start of a match, a ball will be placed on the scorer's table and one given to each of the ball retrievers nearest the serving areas. These are the only ones authorized to give the ball to the server.*

   c) *When the ball is outside the playing areas, it should be recovered by one of the ball retrievers and given to the one who has already given the ball to the player who will make the next service; (2) If the ball is on the court, the player nearest the ball should immediately place it outside the court.*

   d) *At the instant the ball is ruled dead, the ball retriever nearest the service area will quickly give the ball to the player who will be executing the next service. Players may not give the ball to the server.*

   e) *During a time-out, the first referee may authorize the second referee to give the ball to the retriever nearest the area where the next service will occur.*

   f) *A ball being returned from one ball retriever to another will be rolled, not thrown, along the floor outside the court. A ball being returned should be delivered to the ball retriever who has just given a ball to the server.*

CHAPTER II
PARTICIPANTS IN COMPETITION

RULE 4. RIGHTS AND DUTIES OF PLAYERS AND TEAM PERSONNEL

Article 1. RULES OF THE GAME—All coaches and players are required to know the rules of the game and abide by them.

Article 2. DISCIPLINE OF TEAM—The coaches, managers and captains are responsible for discipline and proper conduct of their team personnel.

Article 3. SPOKESMAN OF THE TEAM—The playing captain is the only player who may address the first referee and shall be the spokesman of the team. The captains may also address the second referee, but only on matters concerning the captain's duties. The designated head coach may address the referees only for the purpose of requesting a time-out or substitution.

Article 4. TIME-OUT REQUESTS — Requests for time-out may be made by the designated head coach and/or the playing captain when the ball is dead.

a) Each team is allowed two time-outs in each game. Consecutive time-outs may be requested by either team without the resumption of play between time-outs. The length of a time-out is limited to 30 seconds.

b) If a team captain or head coach inadvertantly requests a third time-out, it shall be refused and the team warned. If, in the judgement of the first referee, a team requests a third time-out as a means of attempting to gain an advantage, the offending team will be penalized with loss of service, or if not serving, the opponents shall be awarded a point.

c) During a time-out, the players are not allowed to leave the court and may not speak to anyone except to receive advice from one coach who may stand near, but not on the court.

d) A team attendant may approach the players on the court for the purpose of providing water, towels, medical assistance, etc., but must move back from the side of the court when not engaged in administering such duties.

NOTE: NAGWS rules provide that either the head coach or the assistant coach may request a time-out. During a time-out, two persons may approach the side of the court and both may speak to the players on the court.

Article 5. TEAM BENCHES — Benches are to be placed on the right and left of the scorer's table. Team members shall occupy the bench located on the side of the net adjacent to their playing area. Only the coaches, a trainer, a doctor or masseur and the reserve players can be seated on such benches. Coaches shall be seated on end of the bench nearest the scorer's table.

Article 6. ACTS SUBJECT TO SANCTION — The following acts of coaches, players, substitutes and other team members are subject to sanction:

a) Addressing of officials concerning their decisions.

b) Making profane or vulgar remarks or acts to officials, opponents or spectators.

c) Committing actions tending to influence decisions of officials.

d) Coaching during the game by any team member from outside the court.

e) Crossing the vertical plane of the net with any part of the body with the purpose of distracting an opponent while the ball is in play.

f) Shouting or yelling in such a manner as to distract an opponent who is playing, or attempting to play, a ball.

g) Leaving the court during an interruption of play in the game without the permission of the first referee.

h) It is forbidden for teammates to clap hands at the instant of contact with the ball by a player, particularly during the reception of a service.

i) Shouting or taking any action conducive to distracting the first referee's judgement concerning handling of the ball.

Article 7. SANCTIONS — Offenses committed by coaches, players and/or other team members may result in the following warning, penalty, expulsion from the game or disqualification from the match:

a) WARNING: For minor unsportsmanlike offenses, such as talking to opponents, spectators or officials, shouting or unintentional acts that cause a delay in the game, a warning (yellow card) is issued and is recorded on the scoresheet. A second minor offense must result in a penalty.

b) PENALTY: For rude behavior or a second minor offense, a penalty (red card) is issued by the first referee and is recorded on the scoresheet. A penalty automatically entails the loss of service by the offending team if serving, or if not serving, the awarding of a point to the opponents. A second act warranting the issue of a penalty by the first referee results in the expulsion of a player.

c) EXPULSION: Offensive conduct (such as obscene or insulting words or gestures) towards officials, spectators or opponents, results in expulsion of a player from the game (red and yellow cards together). A second expulsion during a match must result in the disqualification of a player or team member.

d) DISQUALIFICATION: A second expulsion during a match or any attempted or actual physical aggression towards an official, spectator or opponent results in the disqualification of a player or team member for the remainder of a match (red and yellow cards apart). Disqualified persons must leave the area (including spectator area) of the match.

COMMENTARY ON RULE 4
RIGHTS AND DUTIES OF PLAYERS AND TEAM PERSONNEL

1) *REFEREE RESPONSIBILITY— The first referee is responsible for the conduct of the coaches, players and other team personnel. Under no circumstances will the first referee allow incorrect or unsportsmanlike behavior or rude remarks.*
   a) *Only the first referee is empowered to warn, penalize or disqualify a member of a team.*
   b) *If the captain asks in a proper manner, the first referee must give the reason for a penalty or disqualification and must not allow any further discussion.*
      1) *Should there be a disagreement pertaining to a sanction assessed by the referee, team captains may state their case in writing on the scoresheet after completion of the match.*

2) *HEAD COACH — One person on the team roster must be designated as the head coach. That person may request time-outs or substitutions when not in the game as a player, or when in the game as a player if designated as the playing captain on the lineup sheet. The head coach is responsible for the actions of team members on the bench.*

3) *PLAYING CAPTAIN — One of the six players on the court shall be designated as the playing captain. The captain designated on the lineup sheet submitted at the start of the game shall remain the playing captain at all times when in the game. When replaced, the captain shall designate another player to assume the duties of captain until replaced or the designated captain returns to the game.*

4) *REPORTING OF RUDE REMARKS — Other officials (second referee, scorer and linesmen) must immediately report to the first referee any rude remark that is made by a player or team member about an official or opponent.*

5) *RECORDING WARNINGS AND PENALTIES — All warnings and actions penalized by loss of service, by a point for the opposite team or the disqualification of a*

player or team member for a game or match, must be recorded on the scoresheet.

6) CONDUCT BETWEEN GAMES — Minor unsportsmanlike behavior between games of a match is ignored. If the behavior is of sufficient nature (such as a derogatory remark or act), the first referee may expel a player or team member from the next game or may disqualify them from the remainder of a match. No penalty, other than expulsion or disqualification, will be assessed between games of a match.

7) DISQUALIFICATION — If the first referee feels that a player or team member has committed a serious unsportsmanlike act that warrants disqualification from more than the match in which the act was discovered, a report must be made to the authority in charge of the tournament for final action. First referees are authorized to disqualify players for one match only. Disqualification does not carry any further penalty (i.e., point, side-out, time-out). Disqualified personnel must immediately leave the area of the match, including any spectator areas.

8) TEAM BENCHES — Coaches, substitutes and any other team members not playing in the game shall remain seated on the team bench unless requesting a time-out, requesting a substitution, warming up preparatory to entering a game, a substitute reporting to the scorer, trainers or doctors assisting a player on the bench, coaching duties requiring discussion with a player on the bench, periods between games of a match or other such times as authorized by the first referee. Team members shall occupy the bench located on the side of the net adjacent to their playing area and shall immediately change benches when the teams change in the middle of a deciding game of a match. The designated head coach, or person in charge of the conduct of players on the bench if the head coach is playing or has been disqualified, shall occupy the seat nearest the scorer's table.

9) COACHING — A coach during sanctioned USVBA competition, except Junior teams in Junior competition, may not give instructions to players during the match and may not argue or protest to the referees. Coaches, substitutes and other team members shall be seated on the team bench during play. Coaches may rise and stand in front of the team bench for the purpose of

a) Requesting a time-out or substitution.

b) Reacting spontaneously to an outstanding play by a member of the team.

c) Attending an injured player when beckoned onto the court by a referee.

d) Conferring with substitutes or other personnel on the team bench.

e) Conferring with players at the side of the court during a charged time-out.

The same applies, throughout the match, to all persons located on the team bench.

On the first occasion, if such a fault occurs in any one game, the first referee must warn the team concerned. On the second occasion, a penalty is given and noted on the scoresheet and the team at fault penalized by loss of service or the opponent gains a point. NOTE: Non-disruptive coaching will be permitted in NAGWS and Inter-Collegiate competition.

10) TIME-OUT PERIODS — If a captain or coach of either team asks the second referee for a time-out after the first referee has blown the whistle for service, the second referee must refuse the request. If, however, the second referee blows the whistle and play is stopped, the team making the request shall not be penalized, but the request will be denied and the first referee shall direct a playover.

a) Teams granted a legal time-out may terminate the time-out period at any time they indicate that they are ready to resume play. If the opponents wish to extend the time-out period, that team shall be charged with a team time-out.

b) If a team fails to return to play immediately upon the signal indicating the end of a time-out period, that team shall be charged a time-out. If such time-out is the first or second time-out charged the team, the team may use the 30 seconds. If such delay is after a team has used its two time-outs, the team shall be penalized (point or side out) and may not use the 30 seconds.

c) If a team makes a third request for time-out, the request shall be refused and the team warned by the first referee. If the request is inadvertantly granted, the time-out shall be terminated immediately upon discovery and the team warned. Any additional requests shall result in a penalty (point or side out). If, in the first referee's opinion, a third request for time-out is made as a means of gaining an advantage, it shall be charged as a serious offense and the team penalized (point or side out).

d) If a player or team member, other than the designated coach or playing captain, requests a time-out, the request will be denied and the team warned. If the request results in the granting of a time-out, it shall be terminated immediately upon discovery of the illegal request and the team warned.

11) CONDUCT DURING GAME—During play, if a player shouts or yells at an opponent or crosses the vertical plane of the net for the purpose of distracting an opponent, the first referee shall:

a) If the distraction does not cause a fault or hinder play, wait until the conclusion of the play and then warn the player, or;

b) If the distraction causes a fault or hinders play of an opponent, immediately stop play and penalize the player for serious unsportsmanlike conduct.

RULE 5. THE TEAMS

Article 1. PLAYERS' UNIFORMS—The playing uniform shall consist of jersey, shorts and light and pliable shoes (rubber or leather soles without heels).

a) It is forbidden to wear a head gear or any article (jewelry, pins, bracelets, etc.) which could cause injuries during the game. If requested by a team captain before the match commences, the first referee may grant permission for one or more players to play without shoes.

b) Players' jerseys must be marked with numbers 8 to 15 cm. (3" to 6") in height on the chest and 15 to 24 cm. (6" to 9") in height on the back. The width of the strip forming the number shall be 2 cm. (3/4") in international matches. The captain in international competition shall wear a badge on the left side of the chest 8 cm. by 1.5 cm. (3" by 1/2") in a color different to that of the jersey.

c) Members of a team must appear on the court dressed in clean presentable uniforms (jerseys and shorts) of the same color, style, cut and trim. For the purpose of identical uniforms, shoes and socks are not considered a part of the uniform and are not required to be identical for team members. During cold weather, it is permissable for teams to wear identical training suits provided they are numbered in accordance with the specifications of paragraph b) above and are of the same color, style, cut and trim.

Article 2. COMPOSITION OF TEAMS AND SUBSTITUTIONS — A team shall consist of six players regardless of circumstances. The composition of a complete team, including substitutes, may not exceed twelve players.

a) Before the start of a match, teams shall give the scorer a roster listing all players, including substitutes, and the uniform number each player will wear. Rosters shall also indicate the designated head coach. Once the roster has been received by the scorer, no changes may be made.

b) Prior to the start of each game of a match, the head coach or captain shall submit to the scorer a lineup of players who will be starting the game and the position in the service order each will play. Lineups will be submitted on the official lineup sheets provided by the scorer. After the lineup sheets have been received by the scorer, no changes may be made unless necessitated due to a scorer error or omission. Players listed on the lineup sheets may be replaced prior to the start of play through a substitution request by the team coach or captain under the provisions of paragraph e) below. One of the players on the lineup sheet must be designated as the playing captain. Opponents will not be permitted to see the lineup submitted by the opposing team prior to the start of play.

c) Substitutes and coaches must be on the side of the court opposite the first referee and shall remain seated during play. Substitutes may warm up outside the playing area providing they do not use a ball and that they return to their designated places afterwards if not immediately entering the game.

d) Substitution of players may be made when the ball is dead, on the request of either the playing captain on the court or the designated head coach off the court and when recognized by either referee. A team is allowed a maximum of six (6) team substitutions in any one game. Before entering the game, a substitute must report to the second referee in proper playing uniform and be ready to enter upon the floor when authorization is given. If the requested substitution is not completed immediately, the team will be charged with a time-out and shall be allowed to use such time-out unless it has already used the allowable number of time-outs. In case the team has already exhausted the allowable two time-outs, the team shall be penalized by loss of service or, if not serving, the opponents shall be awarded a point.

e) The captain or coach requesting a substitution(s) shall indicate the number of substitutions desired and shall report to the scorer and second referee the numbers of players involved in the substitution. If the coach or captain fails to indicate that more than one substitution is desired, the first or second referee shall refuse any additional substitute(s) until the next legal opportunity. Following a completed substitution, a team may not request a new substitution until play has resumed and the ball is dead again or until a time-out has been requested and granted to either team. During a legal charged time-out, any number of requests for substitution may be made by either team. Immediately following a time-out, an additional request for substitution may be made.

f) A player starting a game may be replaced only once by a substitute and may subsequently enter the game once, but in the original position in the serving order in relation to other teammates. Only the original starter may replace a substitute during the same game. There may be a maximum of two players participating in any one position in the service order (except in case of accident or injury requiring abnormal substitution under the provisions of paragraph h) below). If an illegal substitution request is made (i.e., excess player entry, excess team substitution, wrong position entry, etc.) the request will be refused and the team charged a time-out. At the expiration of the time-out period, if a substitution is still desired, a new request must be made.

g) If a player becomes injured and cannot continue playing within 10 to 15 seconds, such player must be replaced. After that brief period, if the team desires to have the player remain in the game, and if the player cannot continue to play immediately, the team must use a charged time-out. If the player is replaced, regardless of time required to safely remove the player from the court, no time-out shall be charged.

h) If through accident or injury a player is unable to play and substitution cannot be made under the provisions of paragraph f), or if the team has used its allowable six (6) team substitutions, such player may be replaced in the following priority without penalty:
(1) By any substitute who has not participated in the game.
(2) By the player who played in the position of the injured player.
(3) By any substitute, regardless of position previously played.
Players removed from the game under the abnormal substitution provisions of paragraph h) will not be permitted to participate in the remainder of the game.

i) If through injury or accident a player is unable to play and substitution cannot be made under the provisions of paragraphs f) and h), the referee may grant a special time-out of up to three (3) minutes. Play will be resumed as soon as the injured player is able to continue. In no case shall the special injury time-out exceed three minutes. At the end of the special time-out, a team may request a normal time-out charged to that team provided they have not already used their allowable two (2) time-outs. If, after three minutes, or at the expiration of time outs granted subsequent to the special time-out, the injured player cannot continue to play, the team loses the game by default, keeping the points acquired.

NOTE: Senior Division and NAGWS competition will be governed by the special provisions set forth in Current Practices for Rule 5.

j) If a team becomes incomplete through disqualification of a player, and substitution cannot be made under the provisions of paragraph f) above, the team loses the game by default, keeping the points acquired.

COMMENTARY ON RULE 5
THE TEAMS

1) *NUMBER OF PLAYERS — Each player must wear a number on the front and back of the shirt while participating in the game. The shirts may be numbered between 1 and 15 inclusive for international competition. For USVBA competition, shirts may be numbered between 1 and 99 inclusive. No player shall participate without a legal number. No player shall change numbers during a match without permission of the first referee.*

2) COLORS — When opponents have jerseys of the same color, it occasionally creates confusion as to the player who has committed a fault and the team for whom the player plays. Therefore, the home team should change colors if possible.

3) JEWELRY AND OTHER ARTICLES — Rings, with the exception of flat bands without projections, bracelets, dangling earrings and necklaces long enough to clear the chin must be removed. Necklaces of multi-piece construction (beads, etc.) must also be removed due to possible breakage that could result in a delay in the game. If an article cannot be removed, it must be taped securely to allow the player to play. Braided hair with beads must be secured so that it will not present a safety hazard to the player, teammates or opponents. Hair barrettes may be used to secure the hair. It is not necessary that the barrettes be taped. If play must be stopped to allow a player to remove illegal jewelry or equipment, that team shall be charged with a time-out. If the team has not used its allowable two time-outs, they may use the time. If they have used their allowable two time-outs, they shall be penalized (point or side out) and may not use the time.

a) The wearing of a hard cast of any nature, hard splint, or other type of potentially dangerous protective device shall be prohibited, regardless of how padded. The wearing of a soft bandage to cover a wound or protect an injury shall be permitted. The wearing of an "air-filled" type cast on the lower extremities may be permitted.

b) "Head-gear" is interpreted to mean no hats or bandanas. A sweat band of soft pliable material or bandana folded and worn as a sweat band is permissible.

4) LOW TEMPERATURE — If the temperature is low (about 10 deg. centigrade; 50 deg. farenheit), the first referee may allow players to wear sweatsuits provided they are all of the same style and color and are legally numbered in accordance with the provision of Rule 5, Article 1.

5) REQUIRED NUMBER OF PLAYERS — Under no circumstances may a team play with less than six (6) players.

6) SUBSTITUTIONS — Only the head coach designated on the roster, or the playing captain on the court, may ask the referees for permission to make a substitution.

a) Substitutes must be already standing so that the replacement can be made immediately when authorized by the second referee.

b) The captain or head coach must first announce the number of substitutions desired and then the numbers of the players exchanging positions. Failure to indicate that multiple substitution is desired shall limit the team to one substitute. In the event that more than one player attempts to enter, such player(s) will be refused entry and the team shall be warned. After making a request and indicating the number of substitutions desired, if the head coach or captain refuses to complete the substitution or reduces the number of substitutions to be made, the team shall be charged with a time-out. If the time-out is the first or second charged to the team, the team may use the 30 seconds. At the expiration of the time-out period, if a substitution is still desired, a new request must be made. If the time-out results in a third charged time-out, the team shall be penalized (point or side out) and may not use the 30 seconds. (EXCEPTION: If the change in request is due to a referee's mind change, the request will be honored and no time-out shall be charged)

c) *Substitutes going on the court must raise one hand and wait by the side of the court in the designated substitution zone until permission is given by the second referee for the exchange to be made. Players leaving the court must raise one hand and touch the hand of the substitute entering the court. Such procedure allows the scorer to correctly identify the players who are exchanging positions.*

d) *If a player or team member, other than the captain or designated coach, makes a request for substitution, the request shall be refused and the team warned by the first referee. If the same act occurs again during the same game, it shall be deemed a serious offense and the team penalized by the first referee.*

e) *Each time a player is replaced, it shall count as an entry for the entering player.*
  (1) *Each player may enter the game a maximum of one time. Starting the game shall not count as an entry.*

f) *Each player entering the game counts against the six substitutions allowed to the team. If the team attempts to make a seventh substitution, the team shall be charged a time-out. Teams may use the 30 seconds unless it results in a third charged time-out. If the time-out results in a third charged time-out, the team shall be penalized and may not use the 30 seconds.*

g) *Players attempting to enter a game an excessive time, in a wrong position or if not listed on the team roster submitted prior to the beginning of a match shall result in the team being charged with a time-out. If the time-out is the first or second charged to the team, the team may use the time. If it is a third charged time-out, the team shall be penalized and may not use the time.*

h) *Players attempting to enter a game after having been expelled, disqualified or replaced under the abnormal substitution rule for injuries shall result in the team being penalized (point or side out) without warning.*

i) *When either referee notices an injured player, play shall be stopped immediately. If the player indicates that play without replacement might be possible, the first referee may allow the player 10 to 15 seconds to make such determination. If play is not possible afer that brief interruption, the player must be replaced or the team must use a charged time-out if the player is to remain in the game.*
  1) *If removal of an injured player causes a delay, no time-out will be charged, regardless of length of time required to safely remove the player from the court. Safety of the player(s) is the primary consideration.*

7) *SUBMITTING LINEUPS — If a team fails to submit a lineup to the scorer before the expiration of the rest period between games of a match, that team shall be charged with a time-out. After an additional 30 seconds, if the lineup has not been submitted, an additional time-out will be charged. The team may use the 30 second time-out periods. If, after the expiration of the second charged time-out, the team has not submitted the lineup, the first referee shall declare a default charged to the offending team.*

a) *Opponents will not be permitted to see the lineup submitted to the scorer by the opposing team prior to the start of play.*

b) *After a lineup has been received by the scorer, no changes may be made in listed players or positions on the court unless a recording error or omission is made by the scorer. Between the submitting of a lineup to the scorer and the start of play for a game or match, teams may request a substitution to replace a player listed on the lineup sheet. Such replacement shall count as both a player and a team substitution. There is no requirement for the replaced player to participate in a play before being replaced. Such requests shall be governed by the provisions of Article 2 e).*

CURRENT PRACTICES FOR RULE 5

1) UNIFORM—Where reference is made to identical uniforms, it is construed to mean only the jerseys and shorts. It is recommended that the lower edges of numerals on the jerseys be at least 4 inches above the waist line and that the color of the numerals be in sharp contrast to that of the uniforms to which they are attached. Reference to home team colors may be ignored.

2) SUBSTITUTIONS FOR SENIOR DIVISION AND NAGWS COMPETITION:

   a) A player shall not enter the game for a fourth time (starting shall count as an entry). A team shall be allowed a maximum of twelve (12) substitutions in any one game. Players starting a game may be replaced by a substitute and may subsequently re-enter the game twice. Each substitute may enter the game three times. Players re-entering the game must assume the original position in the serving order in relation to other teammates. No change shall be made in the order of rotation unless required due to injury requiring abnormal substitution under the provisions of paragraph b) below. Any number of players may enter the game in each position in the service order.

   b) If through accident or injury a player is unable to play, and substitution cannot be made under the provisions of paragraph a), or if the team has used its allowable twelve (12) team substitutions, such player may be replaced in the following priority without penalty:

   (1) By the starter or substitute who has played in the position of the injured player, if such starter or substitute has not already been in the game the allowable three times, or by any player who has not already participated in the game.

   (2) By any player on the bench who has not been in the game three times, regardless of position previously played.

   (3) If all players have been in the game the allowable three times, by the substitute who previously played in the position of the injured player.

   (4) By any substitute, even though all substitutes have been in the game the three allowable times.

   c) If through injury or accident a player is unable to play and substitution cannot be made under the provision of paragraphs a) or b), the first referee may grant a special time-out under the provisions of Rule 5, Article 2 e).

   d) If a team becomes incomplete through disqualification or expulsion of a player and substitution cannot be made under the provision of paragraph a) above, the team loses the game by default, keeping the points acquired.

CHAPTER III
RULES OF PLAY

RULE 6. TEAM AREAS, DURATION OF MATCHES
AND INTERRUPTIONS OF PLAY

Article 1. NUMBER OF GAMES — All International matches shall consist of the best of three out of five games.

Article 2. CHOICE OF PLAYING AREA AND SERVE — The captains will call the toss of a coin for the choice of team area or the service. The winner of the toss chooses: 1. first serve, or; 2. choice of team area for the first game. The loser of the toss receives the remaining option.

Article 3. CHOICE OF PLAYING AREA FOR DECIDING GAME — Before the beginning of the deciding game of a match, the first referee makes a new toss of the coin with the options described in Article 2. The captain of the team not calling the toss of the coin for the first game shall call the toss of the coin for the deciding game.

Article 4. CHANGE OF PLAYING AREAS BETWEEN GAMES — After each game of a match, except when a deciding game is required, teams and team members will change playing area and benches.

Article 5. CHANGE OF PLAYING AREA IN DECIDING GAME OF A MATCH — When teams are tied in number of games won in a match, and one of the teams reaches eight (8) points in a deciding game, the teams will be directed to change playing areas. After change of areas, the serving will continue by the player whose turn it is to serve. In case the change is not made at the proper time, it will take place as soon as it is brought to the attention of the first referee. The score remains unchanged and is not a grounds for protest.

Article 6. TIME BETWEEN GAMES OF A MATCH — A maximum interval of two (2) minutes is allowed between games of a match. Between the fourth and fifth games of a match, the interval shall be five (5) minutes. The interval between games includes the time required for change of playing areas and submitting of lineups for the next game.

Article 7. INTERRUPTIONS OF PLAY — As soon as the referees notice an injured player, or a foreign object on the court that could create a hazard to a player(s), play will be stopped and the first referee will direct a play-over when play is resumed.

Article 8. INTERRUPTIONS OF THE MATCH — If any circumstances, or series of circumstances, prevent the completion of an International match (such as bad weather, failure of equipment, etc.), the following shall apply:

a) If the game is resumed on the same court after one or several periods, not exceeding four hours, the results of the interrupted game will remain the same and the game resumes under the same conditions as existed before the interruption.

b) If the match is resumed on another court or in another facility, results of the interrupted game will be cancelled. The results of any completed game of the match will be counted. The cancelled game shall be played under the same conditions as existed before the interruption.

c) If the delay exceeds four hours, the match shall be replayed, regardless of where played.

Article 9. DELAYING THE GAME—Any act which, in the judgement of the first referee, unnecessarily delays the game may be penalized (Rule 4, Article 7b).

COMMENTARY ON RULE 6
TEAM AREAS, DURATION OF MATCHES
AND INTERRUPTIONS OF PLAY

1) CHANGING SIDES—Changing sides during the deciding game of a match must be done with a minimum of delay.
   a) No instructions can be given players as they change sides.
   b) Players must assume the same positions they were in before changing team areas.
2) TIME BETWEEN GAMES OF A MATCH—At the expiration of the allowable rest period between games, teams must report immediately to the end line of their playing areas.
   a) If a team fails to report to the end line of their playing area immediately upon the signal indicating the expiration of the period between games, that team shall be charged with a time-out. After an additional 30 seconds, if the team has failed to report to the end line, the team shall be charged with an additional time-out. The team may use the 30 second time-out periods. If, after the expiration of the second charged time-out, the team has not reported to the end line, the first referee shall declare a default charged to the offending team. Score of the defaulted game shall be recorded at 15-0.
   b) A two minute period shall begin immediately after a game has been declared defaulted by the first referee. During the two minute period, teams shall change sides and submit lineups for the next scheduled game.
   c) If the same team again fails to report to the end line within the provisions of (a) above, the match shall be declared a default by the first referee. A defaulted match shall be recorded as 2-0 or 3-0, depending upon the number of games scheduled.
3) DELAYING THE GAME—In order to clarify the interpretation of Rule 6, Article 9, it is necessary to explain that any attempt to delay the game shall result in a warning from the first referee. If the attempt is repeated, or it is determined that the attempt is deliberate by a player or team, the referee must penalize the team or player by denoting it a serious offense (Rule 4, Article 7b).

CURRENT PRACTICES FOR RULE 6

1) ONE GAME PLAYOFF—A one game playoff shall be considered as a deciding game of a match and the teams shall change sides when one team has scored eight points.
2) MATCHES WITHOUT DECIDING GAMES—In the interest of consistency, a toss of the coin should be held prior to a third or fifth game of a match in which such games will be played regardless of outcome of preceding games of the match.
   a) In the final game of a three or five game match where all games are played, regardless of outcome, teams will change playing areas when one team has scored its eighth point.

3) TIME GAME—In circumstances where the efficient management of a tournament or series of matches requires adherence to a time schedule in order to complete the competitions, the time game may be employed. Such time games may
be played on the basis of ball-in-play-game or 15 points, whichever occurs first.
Such basis must be established before the first game where round robins, a
specific number of games, etc., are indicated as the format.

RULE 7. COMMENCEMENT OF PLAY AND THE SERVICE

Article 1. THE SERVICE—The service is the act of putting the ball into play by the
player in the right back position who hits the ball with the hand (open or closed) or any
part of the arm in an effort to direct the ball into the opponent's area.
a) The server shall have five seconds after the first referee's readiness to serve whistle
in which to release or toss the ball for service.
b) After being clearly released or thrown from the hand(s) of the server, the ball shall
be cleanly hit for service. (EXCEPTION: If, after releasing or throwing the ball for
service, the server allows the ball to fall to the floor (ground) without being hit or
contacted, the service effort shall be cancelled and a replay directed. However, the
referee will not allow the game to be delayed in this manner more than one time
during any service).
c) At the instant the ball is hit for the service, the server shall not have any portion of
the body in contact with the end line, the court or the floor (ground) outside the
lines marking the service area. At the instant of service, the server may stand on or
between the two lines, or their extensions which mark the service area.
d) The service is considered good if the ball passes over the net between the antennas
or their indefinite extensions without touching the net or other objects.
e) If the ball is served before the first referee's whistle, the serve shall be cancelled
and a re-serve directed. The first referee will not allow a player to delay the game
in this manner more than one time.
Article 2. SERVING FAULTS—The referee will signal side-out and direct a change of
service to the other team when one of the following serving faults occurs:
a) The ball touches the net.
b) The ball passes under the net.
c) The ball touches an antenna or does not pass over the net completely between the
antennas or their indefinite extensions.
d) The ball touches a player of the serving team or any object before entering the opponent's playing area.
e) The ball lands outside the limits of the opponent's playing area.
Article 3. DURATION OF SERVICE—A player continues to serve until a fault is committed by the serving team.
Article 4. SERVING OUT OF ORDER—If a team has served out of order, the team
loses the service and any points gained during such out of order service. The players of
the team at fault must immediately resume their correct positions on the court.
Article 5. SERVICE IN SUBSEQUENT GAMES—The team not serving first in the
preceding game of a match shall serve first in the next game of the match, except in
the deciding game of a match (Rule 6, Article 3).

Article 6. CHANGE OF SERVICE — The team which receives the ball for service shall rotate one position clockwise before serving.

Article 7. SCREENING — The players of the serving team must not, through screening, prevent their opponents from watching the server or the trajectory of the ball.

a) Any player on the serving team who has hands clearly above the height of the head, extends arms sideward, moves the arms to distract the opponents, jumps or moves sideways, etc., while the serve is being effected, is guilty of making an individual screen.

b) A team makes a group screen when the server is hidden behind a group of two or more teammates and the ball is served over them in the direction of the opponents.

Article 8. POSITIONS OF PLAYERS AT SERVICE — At the time the ball is contacted for the serve, the placement of players on the court must conform to the service order recorded on the scoresheet as follows (the server is exempt from this requirement):

a) In the front line, the center forward (3) may not be as near the right sideline as the right forward (2) nor as near the left sideline as the left forward (4). In the back line, the center back (6) may not be as near the right sideline as the right back (1) nor as near the left sideline as the left back (5). No back line player may be as near the net as the corresponding front line player. After the ball is contacted for the serve, players may move from their respective positions.

b) The serving order as recorded on the official scoresheet must remain the same until the game is completed.

c) Before the start of a new game, the serving order may be changed and such changes must be recorded on the scoresheet. It is the responsibility of the head coach or team captain to submit a lineup to the scorer prior to the expiration of the authorized rest period between games of a match.

Article 9. ERROR IN POSITION OR ILLEGAL PLAYER IN GAME — When a player(s) of a team is found to be illegally in the game or has entered in a wrong position in the service order, the play must be stopped and the error corrected. A red card penalty shall be issued to the player(s) at fault by the first referee and the following corrective action taken:

a) If discovered before a service by the opponents, all points scored by the team while any player(s) was illegally in the game or in a wrong position in the service order shall be cancelled. If the team at fault is serving at the time of discovery of the error, a side out will be declared.

b) If the team at fault is not serving at the time of discovery of the error, all points scored by the opponents will be retained. The serving team shall be awarded a point unless discovery of the error is immediately following a play in which the serving team scored a point. In such case, no additional point will be awarded. The wrong position will be corrected and play continued without further penalty.

c) If it is not possible to determine when the error first occurred, the first referee shall issue a red card to the player(s) at fault and the team in error shall resume the correct position(s) and, if serving, shall have a side out declared against it. If the other team is serving, it shall be awarded a point unless the play immediately preceding discovery of the error in position or player illegally in the game resulted in a point.

d) If correction of the error requires a substitution due to an illegal or wrong position entry of a player(s), neither the team or player(s) will be charged with a substitution.

In addition, any player or team substitutions charged at the time of the wrong entry shall be removed from the scoresheet as though they had never occurred.

COMMENTARY ON RULE 7
COMMENCEMENT OF PLAY AND THE SERVICE

1) *THE SERVICE — If the server releases or tosses the ball for service, but does not hit it and it touches some part of the server's body as it falls, this counts as a fault and the ball shall be given to the other team.*
   a) *If the server releases the ball preparatory to serving, but allows it to fall to the floor (ground) without touching it, the first referee shall cancel the serve and direct a second and last attempt at service (replay) for which an additional five seconds is allowed. If the player does not serve within these time limits, a serious offense is committed which must be penalized by loss of service.*
   b) *The server is not allowed to delay service after the first referee's whistle, even if it appears that players on the serving team are in a wrong position or are not ready.*
   c) *Service cannot be made with two hands or arms.*
   d) *At the moment of service, the server's body may be in the air entirely forward of the end line provided the last contact with the floor (ground) was within the legal service area.*
   e) *If a service fault occurs (Rule 7, Article 2) and the opposing team commits a positional fault at the moment of service (Rule 7, Article 8), the server's team scores a point.*
   f) *If an illegal service occurs and the opposing team commits a positional fault at the moment of service, the ball is given to the opponents. The service is illegal when:*
      (1) *The player serves while in contact with the floor (ground) outside the service area.*
      (2) *The ball is thrown or pushed for service.*
      (3) *The player serves with two hands or arms.*
      (4) *The service is not made following the correct rotational order.*
      (5) *The ball is not thrown or released before it is hit for service.*
      (6) *Service actions not initiated within five seconds after the first referee's readiness-to-serve whistle.*
2) *SCREENING — In order for members of the serving team to be called for a group screen at the moment of service, the ball must be served in such a manner that it passes over at least two members of the serving team, including players who are in the act of switching positions. The mere grouping of players close together does not constitute a screen unless the ball passes over them. If a single player of the serving team raises the hands clearly above the height of the head, extends arms to the side, jumps or moves sideways at the moment of service, such player shall be charged with a fault for an individual screen, regardless of the path of the ball.*
   a) *If a member of the serving team deliberately takes a position in front of an opponent for the purpose of screening the action of the server, or if the opponent*

moves and the member of the serving team also moves to a position in front of the opponent, the player shall be penalized (red card) for unsportsmanlike conduct.

b) If, in the opinion of the first referee, a player jumps from the floor for the purpose of distracting an opponent immediately after the ball has been contacted for service, such player shall be guilty of unsporting conduct and a sanction shall be imposed by the first referee.

3) POSITION OF PLAYERS — The position of players is judged according to the position of their feet in contact with the floor (ground) at the time the ball is contacted for service. For the purpose of this rule, the service area is not considered to be a part of the court. All players, except the server, must be fully on the court at the time the ball is contacted for service. Players in contact with the center line are governed by the provisions of Rule 9, Article 6. At the instant the server hits the ball for service, all players must be in their proper positions corresponding with the order noted on the scoresheet. The server is exempt from the rule governing the positions of players on the court at service (Rule 7, Article 8). A positional fault should be signalled by the referee(s) as soon as the ball has been hit by the server.

a) Occasionally there may be doubt as to whether a player is a front or back line player. In such cases, the referee may withhold the whistle and check the lineup sheet after the play has been concluded. If a check of the lineup sheet reveals that a player was out of position, the call may be made, even though late.

4) WRONG SERVER — When it is discovered that a wrong player is about to serve the ball, the scorer shall wait until the service has been completed and then blow the horn/whistle or stop the game in any manner possible and report the fault to one of the referees. Any points scored by a wrong player shall be removed, a side-out declared and players of the team at fault must immediately resume their correct positions on the court.

CURRENT PRACTICES FOR RULE 7

1) PRELIMINARY SERVICE ACTION — Preliminary actions, such as bouncing the ball on the floor or lightly tossing the ball from one hand to the other, shall be allowed, but shall be counted as part of the five seconds allowed for the server to initiate service release or toss the ball preparatory for the service.

2) SERVICE FOR ELEMENTARY GRADE PLAYERS — Where elementary grade age players are in a competition, it can be considered legal service if the ball is hit directly from the hand of the server, not necessarily dropped or tossed. Where this serve is acceptable, it should be established in advance or otherwise agreed upon mutually before competition starts and the officials notified. In such levels of team play, players should be encouraged to develop ability and skills necessary for a serve which does satisfy the requirements of the official rule.

3) REQUESTING LINEUP CHECK — Team captains may request verification of the service order of their team if done on an infrequent basis. Requests for lineup checks for opponents will be limited to determining whether or not the players are legally in the game. No information will be provided to disclose which opposing players are front line or back line players.

RULE 8. PLAYING THE BALL

Article 1. MAXIMUM OF THREE TEAM CONTACTS—Each team is allowed a maximum of three (3) successive contacts of the ball in order to return the ball to the opponent's area. (EXCEPTION: Rule 8, Article 11)

Article 2. CONTACTED BALL—A player who contacts the ball, or is contacted by the ball, shall be considered as having played the ball.

Article 3. CONTACT OF BALL WITH THE BODY—The ball may be hit with any part of the body on or above the waist.

Article 4. SIMULTANEOUS CONTACTS WITH THE BODY—The ball can contact any number of parts of the body down to and including the waist providing such contacts are simultaneous and that the ball rebounds immediately and cleanly after such contact.

Article 5. DOUBLE CONTACT—A player contacting the ball more than once with whatever part of the body, without any other player having touched it between these contacts, will be considered as having committed a double hit. Such contacts are a fault. (EXCEPTION: Rule 8, Article 11)

Article 6. HELD BALL—When the ball visibly comes to rest momentarily in the hands or arms of a player, it is considered as having been held. The ball must be hit in such a manner that it rebounds cleanly after contact with a player. Scooping, lifting, pushing or carrying the ball shall be considered to be a form of holding. A ball clearly hit with one or both hands from a position below the ball is considered a good play.

Article 7. SIMULTANEOUS CONTACTS BY OPPONENTS—If the ball is held simultaneously by two opposing players, it is a double fault and the first referee will direct a play-over.

a) If the ball is contacted simultaneously by opponents and is not held, play shall continue.

b) After simultaneous contact by opponents, the team on whose side the ball falls shall have the right to play the ball three times.

c) If, after simultaneous contact by opponents, the ball falls out of bounds, the team on the opposite side shall be deemed as having provided the impetus necessary to cause the ball to be out of bounds.

Article 8. BALL PLAYED BY TEAMMATES—When two players of the same team contact the ball simultaneously, this is considered as two team contacts and neither of the players may make the next play on the ball. (EXCEPTION: Rule 8, Article 11)

Article 9. ATTACKING OVER OPPONENT'S COURT—A player is not allowed to attack the ball on the opposite side of the net. If the ball is hit above the spiker's side of the net and then the follow-through causes the spiker's hand and arm to cross the net without contacting an opponent, such action does not constitute a fault.

Article 10. ASSISTING A TEAMMATE—No player shall assist a teammate by holding such player while the player is making a play on the ball. It shall be legal for a player to hold a teammate not making a play on the ball in order to prevent a fault.

Article 11. BLOCKING—Blocking is the action close to the net which intercepts the ball coming from the opponent's side by making contact with the ball before it crosses the net, as it crosses the net or immediately after it has crossed the net. An attempt to block does not constitute a block unless the ball is contacted during the effort. A blocked ball is considered to have crossed the net.

a) Blocking may be legally accomplished by only the players who are in the front line at the time of service.
b) Multiple contacts of the ball by a player(s) participating in a block shall be legal provided it is during one attempt to intercept the ball.
   (1) Multiple contacts of the ball during a block shall be counted as a single contact, even though the ball may make multiple contacts with one or more players of the block.
c) Any player participating in a block shall have the right to make the next contact, such contact counting as the first of three hits allowed the team.
d) The team which has effected a block shall have the right to three additional contacts after the block in order to return the ball to the opponent's.
e) Back line players may not block or participate in a block, but may play the ball in any other position near or away from the block.
f) Blocking of the ball across the net above the opponent's court shall be legal provided that such block is:
   (1) After a player of the attacking team has served, spiked the ball, or, in the first referee's judgement, intentionally directed the ball into the opponent's court.
   (2) After the opponents have completed their allowable three hits; or,
   (3) After the opponents have hit the ball in such a manner that the ball would, in the first referee's judgement, clearly cross the net if not touched by a player, provided no member of attacking team is in a position to make a legal play on the ball; or,
   (4) If the ball is falling near the net and no member of the attacking team could reasonably make a play on the ball.

Article 12. BALL CONTACTING TOP OF NET AND BLOCK—If the ball touches the top of the net and a player(s) participating in a block and then returns to the attacker's side of the net, this team shall then have the right of three more contacts to return the ball to the opponent's area.

Article 13. BACK LINE ATTACKER—A back line player returning the ball to the opponent's side while forward of the attack line must contact the ball when at least part of the ball is below the level of the top of the net over the attacking team's area. The restriction does not apply if the back line player jumps from clearly behind the attack line and, after contacting the ball, lands on or in front of that line.
a) A player commits a fault when, as a back line player, he/she is in the front zone or touching the attack line, or its imaginary extension, and hits the ball while it is completely above the height of the net and if the ball crosses directly and completely the vertical plane of the net.

COMMENTARY ON RULE 8
PLAYING THE BALL

1) RECEPTION OF THE BALL—*Contact with the ball must be brief and instantaneous. When the ball has been hit hard, or during setting action, it sometimes stays very briefly in contact with the hands of the player handling the ball. In such cases, contact that results from playing the ball from below, or a high reception*

where the ball is received from high in the air, should not be penalized. The following actions of playing the ball should not be counted as faults:
a) When the sound is different to that made by a finger tip hit, but the hit is still
    played simultaneously with both hands and the ball is not held.
b) When the ball is played with two closed fists and the contact with the ball is
    simultaneous.
c) When the ball contacts the open hand and rolls off the hand backward without
    being held.
d) When the ball is played correctly and the player's hands move backwards,
    either during or after the hit.
e) When a poorly hit ball is caused to rotate (such as a defective spike where the
    ball is spun and not hit squarely or a set ball is caused to rotate due to improper
    contact).
2) HELD BALL ON SERVICE RECEIVE—Receiving a served ball with an overhead
    pass using open hands is not necessarily a fault. Such service receives must be
    judged the same as any open handed pass. If the served ball is travelling in a low
    and relatively flat trajectory, receiving it with open hands and passing without
    holding the ball is extremely difficult. If the serve is high and soft, the pass can be
    made legally the same as any similar ball crossing the net after the service.
3) SIMULTANEOUS CONTACTS—The ball may contact several parts of the body at
    the same time legally, provided the ball is not held.
4) DOUBLE CONTACT—Double contact faults are to be judged by sight, not sound.
    Referees must be careful to closely observe contact with the ball and must not let
    unusual body positions or unusual flight of the ball after contact influence their
    determination of a "double-contact".
5) SIMULTANEOUS CONTACT BETWEEN OPPOSING PLAYERS—The rules are
    designed to insure the continuity of play. During contact of the ball simulta-
    neously by opposing players, the first referee must not blow the whistle unless the
    ball is momentarily suspended between the hands of opposing players and clearly
    comes to rest. In such a case, the ball must be replayed without a point or change
    of service being awarded.
6) SIMULTANEOUS CONTACT BETWEEN TEAMMATES—When two players of a
    team attempt to play the ball at the same time, resultant action can cause the ap-
    pearance of simultaneous contact. Referees must be positive that simultaneous
    contact has been seen before charging that team with two hits. If there is any
    doubt, only one hit should be called.
7) ATTACK HIT—A hit by a player in an intentional effort to direct the ball into the
    opponent's court. A third hit by a team is considered to be an attack hit, regardless
    of intention. A served ball is considered to be an attack hit.
8) BLOCKING—Any ball directed towards the opponent's area as an attack hit, in-
    cluding a served ball, can be blocked by one or a group of opposing front line
    players.
a) If members of a composite block are to benefit from the rule allowing multiple
    contacts of the ball by blockers, they must be close to the net and close to each
    other at the time the ball is contacted by the block. If a player is attempting to
    block, but is separated from the block contacted by the ball, such contact will

count as the first of three contacts allowed to return the ball to the opponent's area.

b) Players may take a blocking position with the hands and arms over the net before the opponent's attack hit providing there is no contact with the ball until after the opponents have had an opportunity to play the ball a third time or in action (such as a spike or service) which directs the ball across the net. Immediately after such contact by the attacking team, blockers may contact the ball in an effort to prevent it crossing the net.

c) Multiple contacts of the ball may be made by any player or players taking part in a block and shall constitute one contact of the ball. After such contact, the team is allowed three additional contacts to return the ball to the opponent's area. The multiple contact is legal even if it can be seen that during the blocking action the ball has contacted in rapid succession:

(1) The hands or arms of one player; or,

(2) The hands or arms of two or more players; or

(3) The hands, arms or other parts of one or more players on or above their waists.

d) If the ball touches the top of the net and the hands of an opposing blocker(s), the ball shall be considered to have crossed the net and been blocked. After such contact, the attacking team is allowed an additional three contacts of the ball.

e) Blockers may reach across the plane of the net outside the antenna, but may not contact the ball over the opponent's area. If contact of the ball over the opponent's area is made while any part of the blocker or member of a composite block is outside the antenna across the plane of the net, the block is illegal.

9) BACK LINE PLAYERS—A back line player who is inside the attack zone, or its assumed extension may play the ball directly into the opposite court if, at the moment of contact, the ball is not completely above the level of the top of the net. If a back line player jumps from the floor (ground) clearly behind the attack line, the ball may be spiked or intentionally directed into the opponent's area, regardless of where the player lands after hitting the ball.

a) A ball contacted from above the height of the net (including a spiked ball) and directed towards the opponent's court by a back line player forward of the attack line does not become an illegal hit unless it is the third team hit, the ball passes fully beyond the vertical plane of the net or is legally blocked by the opponents before passing beyond the vertical plane of the net. If the ball is legally blocked by an opponent(s) before crossing the net, the hit by the back line player becomes illegal and the ball becomes dead. If an illegal blocker blocks the ball, it is assumed that the hit became illegal at the moment of contact by the attacker and only the illegal hit shall be penalized.

b) If a back line player at the net, along with the blockers, lifts hands or arms towards the ball as it comes across the net and is touched by the ball, or the ball touches any of the players in that block, it is a fault; back line players not having the right to participate in a block. However, if the block containing the back line player does not touch the ball, the attempt to block is not considered to be a fault.

c) *Back line players may not participate in a block, but there is no restriction on their being next to a block for the purpose of playing the ball in other than blocking action.*

RULE 9. PLAY AT THE NET

Article 1. BALL IN NET BETWEEN ANTENNAS—A ball, other than a served ball, hitting the net between the antennas may be played again. If the ball touches the net after a team's allowable three contacts and does not cross the net, the referee should not stop the play until the ball is contacted for the fourth time or has touched the playing surface. (See Rule 10, Commentary 1)

Article 2. BALL CROSSING THE NET—To be good, the ball must cross the net entirely between the antennas or their assumed indefinite extension.

Article 3. PLAYER CONTACT WITH NET—If a player's action causes the player to contact the net during play, whether accidentally or not, with any part of the player's body or uniform, that player shall be charged with a fault. If the ball is driven into the net with such force that it causes the net to contact a player, such contact shall not be considered a fault.

Article 4. SIMULTANEOUS CONTACT BY OPPONENTS—If opponents contact the net simultaneously, it shall constitute a double fault and the first referee shall direct a replay.

Article 5. CONTACT BY PLAYER OUTSIDE THE NET—If a player accidentally contacts any part of the net supports (e.g. a post, cable), the referee's stand, etc., such contact should not be counted as a fault provided that it has no effect on the sequence of play. Intentional contact or grabbing of such objects shall be penalized as a fault.

Article 6. CROSSING THE CENTER LINE—Contacting the opponent's playing area with any part of the body except the feet is a fault. Touching the opponent's area with a foot or feet is not a fault providing that some part of the encroaching foot or feet remain on or above the center line and does not interfere with the play of an opponent.

a) It is not a fault to enter the opponent's side of the court after the ball has been declared dead by the first referee.

b) It is not a fault to cross the assumed extension of the center line outside the playing area.

  (1) While across the extension of the center line outside the court, a player of the attacking team may play a ball that has not fully passed beyond the plane of the net. Opponents may not interfere with a player making a play on the ball.

  (2) A player who has crossed the extension of the center line and is not making a play on the ball may not interfere with an opponent.

Article 7. BALL PENETRATING OR CROSSING THE VERTICAL PLANE—A ball penetrating the vertical plane of the net over or below the net, whether over or outside the court, may be returned to the attacking team's side by a player of the attacking team provided the ball has not yet completely passed beyond the vertical plane of the net when such contact is made. A ball which has penetrated the vertical plane above the net may be played by either team.

COMMENTARY ON RULE 9
PLAY AT THE NET

1) *BALL CROSSING VERTICAL PLANE OF THE NET*—If a ball penetrates the vertical plane of the net over the net, under the net, or outside the antennas, the attacking team is allowed to attempt to play the ball back into their team area, providing the ball has not fully passed beyond the vertical plane of the net at the time of contact. The opponents are not allowed to intentionally touch the ball under the net during such play. However, if the ball inadvertently contacts an opponent beyond the plane under the net, the ball becomes dead and is not considered to be a fault by the opponents.
   a) Once the ball penetrates the vertical plane above the net, the opponents have equal right to play the ball.
2) *CONTACT WITH OPPONENT'S AREA*—If a player is legally on or above the center line with a foot or feet in contact with the opponent's area, and such foot or feet should cause interference with an opponent who, in the first referee's judgement, could make an immediate subsequent play, it shall be considered a fault. If such contact does not affect play, it shall be ignored.
3) *CONTACT WITH OPPONENT BEYOND THE VERTICAL PLANE*—If a player makes contact with an opponent beyond the vertical plane of the net, and if such contact is inadvertent, the contact shall be ignored unless, in the first referee's judgement, such contact prevents an opponent making a play on the ball. If the contact is intentional, it shall be penalized by the referee without warning.
   a) Flagrant intentional contact shall result in disqualification of the player responsible for the contact.
4) *CROSSING THE CENTER LINE*—It is not a fault to cross the center line onto the opponent's side of the net provided that no contact is made with the opponent's playing area. While across the center line extended, a member of the attacking team is permitted to make a play on the ball provided the ball has not passed fully beyond the vertical plane of the net at the time of contact.
5) *CONTACT WITH POSTS, CABLES, ETC*—If a player accidentally contacts a cable (including the cables supporting the net) or a post, cables supporting a post, referee stand, etc., it should not be counted as a fault unless it directly affects the subsequent sequence of a play. If the stand, posts, etc., are intentionally grasped or used as a means of support, such action constitutes a fault.

RULE 10. DEAD BALL

Article 1. WHEN BALL BECOMES DEAD—A live ball becomes dead when:
a) The ball touches an antenna or the net outside an antenna.
b) The ball does not cross the net completely between the antennas.
c) The ball strikes the floor, wall or any object attached to the wall.
d) The ball contacts the ceiling or object attached to the ceiling at a height of 7 m. or more measured from the playing surface.
e) A player(s) commits a fault.
f) A served ball contacts the net or other object.

g) The first or second referee blows a whistle, even though inadvertently.

h) A player causes the ball to come to rest on a rafter or other overhead object that is less than 7 m. above the height of the playing surface.

COMMENTARY ON RULE 10
DEAD BALL

1) *INADVERTENT WHISTLE — The blowing of an inadvertent whistle causes the ball to become dead immediately. In such cases, the first referee must make a ruling that will not penalize either team. For instance, if the attacking team has hit the ball in such a manner that it is falling in an area where no member of the offensive team could logically make a play on the ball, and if the referee blows the whistle before the ball has touched the playing surface, by rule the ball becomes dead immediately. In this case, the first referee should rule as though the ball had touched the playing surface at the time the whistle blew. Another example should be after a third hit with the ball striking the net near the top and the first referee inadvertently blowing the whistle. After the whistle, if the ball were to roll in such a manner that it crossed the net into the defending team's area, a replay should be called for by the first referee.*

2) *BALL CONTACTING OVERHEAD OBJECT — If the ceiling or other overhead objects attached to the ceiling extend to a height of less than 7 m. above the playing surface, such areas allow the ball to remain in play if struck. However, if the ball strikes such objects and then crosses the vertical plane of the net, the ball becomes dead.*

a) *Some overhead objects, such as basketball baskets protruding from walls or ceilings so that they are within the 2 m. free zone around the court, may be ruled as unfair hampering of the normal play of the ball and may be declared as a replay by the first referee. Also, where objects such as rolled curtains, etc., are suspended over the net, if the first referee feels that such objects unfairly hamper normal play, a replay may be ruled on any ball, other than a served ball, contacting such objects.*

b) *Any special ground rules for a match must be specified in the pre-match conference by the first referee.*

3) *BALL CONTACTING ANTENNA — If the ball contacts the antenna above or below the height of the net, the ball becomes dead.*

RULE 11. TEAM AND PLAYER FAULTS

Article 1. DOUBLE FAULT — A double fault occurs when players of opposing teams simultaneously commit faults. In such cases, the first referee will direct a play over.

Article 2. FAULTS AT APPROXIMATELY THE SAME TIME — If faults by opponents occur at approximately the same time, the first referee shall determine which fault occurred first and shall penalize only that fault. If it cannot be determined which fault occurred first, a double fault shall be declared.

Article 3. PENALTY FOR COMMITTING FAULTS — If the serving team, or a player of the serving team, commits a fault, a side-out shall be declared. If the receiving team, or a player of the receiving team commits a fault, the serving team shall be awarded a point.

Article 4. TEAM AND PLAYER FAULTS—A fault shall be declared against a team or player when:

a) The ball touches the floor (R. 10 A. 1)
b) The ball is held, thrown or pushed (R. 8 A. 6)
c) A team has played the ball more than three times consecutively (R. 8 A. 1)
d) The ball touches a player below the waist (R. 8 A. 3)
e) A player touches the ball twice consecutively (R. 8 A. 5)
f) A team is out of position at service (R. 7 A. 9)
g) A player touches the net or antenna (R. 9 A. 3)
h) A player completely crosses the center line and contacts the opponent's playing area (R. 8 A. 9)
i) A player attacks the ball above the opponent's playing area (R. 8 A. 9)
j) A back line player while in the attack area hits the ball into the opponent's court from above the height of the net (R. 8 A. 9)
k) A ball does not cross the net entirely between the antennas (R. 9 A. 2)
l) A ball lands outside the court or touches an object outside the court (R. 10 A. 1)
m) The ball is played by a player being assisted by a teammate as a means of support. (R. 8 A. 10)
n) A player receives a personal penalty (R. 4 A. 7)
o) A team, after having been warned, receives instructions from coach, manager or substitutes (R. 4 A. 6) NOTE: Non-disruptive coaching is allowed in NAGWS play.
p) A player reaches under the net and touches the ball or an opponent while the ball is being played by the opposite team (R. 9 C. 1)
q) The game is delayed persistently (R. 6 A. 9)
r) An illegal substitution is made (R. 5 A. 2)
s) A team makes a fourth request for time-out after warning (R. 4 A. 4)
t) Extension of a second time-out beyond 30 seconds (R. 4 C. 10)
u) Delay in completing substitution after having used two time-outs (R. 5 A. 2)
v) Player(s), after warning, leaving court during interruption of play without permission of first referee during game (R. 4 A. 4)
w) Players stamp feet or make distracting sounds or gestures towards opponents (R. 4 A. 6)
x) Blocking is performed in an illegal manner (R. 8 A. 11)
y) Illegally served ball or service fault (R. 7 A. 2; R. 7 C. 1f)

RULE 12. SCORING AND RESULTS OF THE GAME

Article 1. WHEN POINT IS SCORED—When a fault is committed by the receiving team, a point is awarded to the serving team.

Article 2. WINNING SCORE—A game is won when a team scores 15 points and has at least a two point advantage over the opponents. If the score is tied at 14-14, the play continues until one team has a lead of two points. (e.g. 16-14, 17-15, 18-16 etc.)

Article 3. SCORE OF DEFAULTED GAME—If a team does not have sufficient players to start a game or refuses to play after the referee requests play to begin, that team shall lose the game by default. Score of each defaulted game will be 15-0.

Article 4. SCORE OF DEFAULTED GAME DUE TO INJURY—If a game is defaulted due to a team being reduced to less than six players because of an injury, the defaulting team shall retain any points earned. The winning team shall be credited with at least 15 points or will be awarded sufficient points to reflect a two point winning advantage over the opponents.

Article 5. SCORE OF DEFAULTED GAME DUE TO EXPULSION OF A PLAYER—If a game is defaulted due to expulsion or disqualification of a player, the defaulting team shall retain any points earned. The offended team shall be credited with at least 15 points or a sufficient number of points to indicate a two point winning advantage over the opponents.

COMMENTARY ON RULE 12
SCORING AND RESULTS OF THE GAME

1) *DEFAULTED GAME* — *If a team defaults a game due to failure to have sufficient players to start a game at the scheduled time, the score will be recorded as 15-0. A waiting time of up to 15 minutes shall be allowed for the team to have sufficient players to play the next game. If the team has at least six players present prior to the expiration of the waiting time, play shall begin. If, after the 15 minute waiting period, a team does not have six players present and ready to play, the second game shall be declared a default. If the match consists of the best 3 out of 5 games, an additional 15 minute waiting period shall be allowed before declaring the match a default.*

    a) *If neither team has six players available at match time, each team shall be charged with a loss by default.*

    b) *Score of each defaulted game is 15-0. Score of a defaulted match is 2-0 or 3-0, depending upon the number of games scheduled to be played.*

2) *REFUSAL TO PLAY* — *If, after receiving a warning from the first referee, a team refuses to play, the game shall be declared a default and recorded as a score of 15-0. A two minute period shall then be granted in order for the teams to change sides of the court and submit lineups for the next game of the match. If the team again refuses to play at the expiration of the two minute period, the match shall be declared a default. A defaulted match shall be recorded as 2-0 or 3-0, depending upon the number of games scheduled to be played.*

RULE 13. DECISIONS AND PROTESTS

Article 1. AUTHORITY OF THE REFEREE—Decisions based on the judgement of the referee or other officials are final and not subject to protest.

Article 2. INTERPRETATION OF THE RULES—Disagreements with interpretations of the rules must be brought to the attention of the first referee prior to the first service following the play in which the disagreement occurred. The captain of the protesting team may be the only one to bring the protest to the attention of the first referee.

Article 3. APPEAL OF DECISION OF THE REFEREE—If the explanation of the first referee following a protest lodged by the team captain is not satisfactory, the captain may appeal to a higher authority. If the protest cannot be resolved, the first referee shall proceed to the scorer's table and shall record, or cause to be recorded, on the scoresheet all pertinent facts of the protest. After the facts of the protest have been recorded, the first referee will continue to direct the game and will forward a report later on the protest in question.

Article 4. DISAGREEMENT WITH REFEREE'S DECISION—If a team captain disagrees with a judgement decision of the referee(s), such decision is not protestable, but the team captain may state such disagreement in writing on the back of the official score-sheet after completion of the match.

COMMENTARY ON RULE 13
DECISIONS AND PROTESTS

1) *PROTEST MATTERS NOT TO BE CONSIDERED*—Protest involving the judge-ment of a referee or other officials will not be given consideration. Some of these items are:
   a) *Whether or not a player on the court was out of position at service.*
   b) *Whether or not a ball was held or thrown.*
   c) *Whether or not a player's conduct should be penalized.*
   d) *Any other matters involving only the accuracy of an official's judgement.*
2) *PROTEST MATTERS TO BE CONSIDERED*—Matters that shall be received and considered by the first referee concern:
   a) *Misinterpretation of a playing rule.*
   b) *Failure of a first referee to apply the correct rule to a given situation.*
   c) *Failure to impose the correct penalty for a given violation.*
3) *RECORDING FACTS*—The following facts should be recorded on the scoresheet concerning any protest situation:
   a) *Score of the game at the time of the protest.*
   b) *Players in the game at the time of the protest and their positions on the court.*
   c) *Player substitutions and team substitutions made prior to the protested situa-tion.*
   d) *Team time-outs charged prior to the protested situation.*
   e) *A synopsis of the situation that caused the protest and the rule violated or omit-ted or the penalty improperly imposed.*
   f) *Signatures of the scorer, both team captains and the first referee, to indicate that the facts have been correctly recorded.*
4) *PROTEST COMMITTEE ACTION*—During the Olympic Games, World Champion-ships and similar competitions, the Jury shall rule upon the protested situation before play continues.
5) *RULING OF THE JURY AND EFFECT*—The Jury, after hearing the facts of the pro-test, may rule that the protest is valid and will be upheld or that the protest is not valid and will be denied. If the protest is upheld, the game will be replayed from the point immediately preceding the play which prompted the lodging of a protest. If the protest is denied, the score and situation will remain as though the protest had never been lodged.

CURRENT PRACTICES FOR RULE 13

1) PROTEST COMMITTEE—Where possible in tournament play, it is advisable to have a protest committee assigned and available to rule upon a protest situation as soon as possible, preferably pior to the first service following the protest. Such action will preclude having to play the match over from the point of protest if the protest is upheld. The situation can be immediately corrected and only the play in question played over.
   a) During sanctioned USVBA competition, the protest committee will rule upon the protested game immediately upon its completion and before another game of the match is played.

CHAPTER IV
OFFICIALS AND THEIR DUTIES

NOTE: Chapter IV is included as a guideline for officials and shall not be construed to be a part of the official playing rules subject to protest by teams.

RULE 14. THE FIRST REFEREE

Article 1. AUTHORITY OF THE FIRST REFEREE—The first referee is in full control of the match and any judgement decisions rendered by the first referee are final. The first referee has authority over all players and officials from the coin toss prior to the first game of a match until the conclúsion of the match, to include any periods during which the match may be temporarily interrupted, for whatever reason.

Article 2. QUESTIONS NOT COVERED BY RULE—The first referee has the power to settle all questions, including those not specifically covered in the rule.

Article 3. POWER TO OVERRULE—The first referee has the power to overrule decisions of other officials when, in the first referee's opinion, they have made errors.

Article 4. POSITION OF FIRST REFEREE DURING MATCH—The first referee shall be located at one end of the net in a position that will allow a clear view of the play. The referee's head should be approximately 50 cm. above the top of the net.

Article 5. PENALIZING VIOLATIONS—In accordance with Rule 4 the first referee penalizes violations made by players, coaches and other team members.

Article 6. USE OF SIGNALS—Immediately after giving a signal to stop play, the first referee shall indicate with the use of hand signals the nature of the violation, if a player fault, the player committing the fault and the team which shall make the next service.

COMMENTARY ON RULE 14
THE FIRST REFEREE

1) SIGNALING SERVICE—The first referee will blow a whistle at the beginning of each play to indicate that service shall begin and at any other time judged to be necessary.

2) *INTERRUPTING PLAY*—Each action is considered finished when the first referee blows a whistle, other than that to indicate service. Generally speaking, the first referee should only interrupt the play when certain that a fault has been committed, and should not blow the whistle if there is any doubt.

3) *REQUESTING ASSISTANCE*—Should the first referee need to deal with anything outside the limits of the court, the first referee should request help from the organizer and players.

4) *OVERRULING OFFICIALS*—If the referee is certain that one of the other officials has made an incorrect decision, the first referee has the power to overrule that official and apply the correct decision. If the first referee feels that one of the other officials is not correctly fulfilling the duties as outlined by the Rules, the referee may have the official replaced.

5) *SUSPENDING THE MATCH*—Should an interruption occur, particularly if spectators should invade the court, the referee must suspend the match and ask the organizers and the captain of the home team to re-establish order within a set period of time. If the interruption continues beyond this period of time, or if one of the teams refuses to continue playing, the first referee must instruct the other officials to leave the court along with the first referee. The first referee must record the incident on the scoresheet and forward a report to the proper authority within 24 hours.

6) *AUTHORITY OF THE REFEREE*—Although the referee is in full control of the match and any judgement decisions rendered are considered final, this in no way relieves the right of team captains to protest and record matters allowed under the provisions of Rule 13, Article 6.

RULE 15. THE SECOND REFEREE

Article 1. POSITION DURING MATCH—The second referee shall take a position on the side of the court opposite and facing the first referee.

Article 2. ASSISTING THE FIRST REFEREE—The second referee shall assist the first referee by making calls such as:

a) Violations of the center line and attack line.

b) Contact with the net by a player.

c) Contact of the ball with an antenna or ball not crossing the net entirely inside the antenna on the second referee's side of the court.

d) Foreign objects entering the court and presenting a hazard to the safety of the players.

e) Performing duties in addition to those outlined when instructed to do so by the first referee.

Article 3. KEEPING OFFICIAL TIME—The second referee shall be responsible for keeping official time of time-outs and rest periods between games of a match.

Article 4. CONDUCT OF PARTICIPANTS—The second referee shall supervise the conduct of coaches and substitutes on the bench and shall call to the attention of first referee any unsportsmanlike actions of players or other team members.

Article 5. SUPERVISION OF SUBSTITUTIONS—The second referee shall authorize substitutions requested by captains or the head coach of the teams.

Article 6. SERVICE ORDER OF TEAMS—The second referee shall verify at the beginning of each game that the positions of the players of both teams correspond with the serving orders listed on the scoresheet and the lineups as given to the scorer. The second referee shall supervise the rotation order and positions of the receiving team at the time of service.

Article 7. GIVING OPINIONS—The second referee shall give opinions on all matters when so requested by the first referee.

Article 8. ENDING PLAY—The play is considered as ended when the second referee blows a whistle.

COMMENTARY ON RULE 15
THE SECOND REFEREE

1) *KEEPING OFFICIAL TIME*—It is the responsibility of the second referee to keep the official time during time-outs, and between games of a match. When a time-out is charged, the second referee will signal the first referee the number of time-outs that have been charged to each team. At the expiration of the time-out, the second referee shall notify the coach or captain the number of time-outs they have taken.

2) *SUBSTITUTIONS*—The second referee will authorize a substitution when the substitute is ready to enter the game. Before allowing the substitute to enter the court, the second referee will make certain that the scorer has the necessary information to properly record the substitution.

3) *CONTROL OF THE BALL*—The second referee shall be responsible for the ball during interruptions of play.

4) *REPLACING FIRST REFEREE*—Should the first referee suddenly be indisposed, it shall be the responsibility of the second referee to assume the responsibilities of the duties of the first referee.

5) *ASSISTING REFEREE*—The second referee will make calls and perform duties in addition to those outlined when instructed to do so by the first referee.

6) *VERIFYING LINEUPS*—It is the duty of the second referee to use the official lineup sheets submitted by the teams to verify that the lineups are correct at the start of a game. When the teams change courts during the middle of a deciding game of a match, it is the duty of the second referee to once again verify that the players of both teams are in their correct service order as listed on the scoresheet.

7) *GIVING INFORMATION TO TEAM CAPTAINS*—Upon request of a team captain for verification that the opponents are in their correct service order or that players are not in the game illegally, the first referee may direct the second referee to verify that the players are correct or incorrect. No direct identification of opposing players will be given to the team captain. Requests for such information by team captains will be limited to infrequent occasions. If it is found that the players are in an incorrect position or illegally in the game, the first referee will direct the second referee and scorer to correct the error.

RULE 16. THE SCORER

Article 1. POSITION DURING MATCH — The scorer's position is on the side of the court opposite the first referee and behind the second referee.

Article 2. RECORDING INFORMATION — Prior to the start of a match, the scorer obtains the lineup sheets and records the names and numbers of the players and substitutes on the scoresheet. Between games of match the scorer reminds the second referee to obtain new lineups from captains or coaches in order to properly record any changes in the lineups. In addition, the scorer:

a) records the score as the match progresses.

b) makes sure that the serving order and rotation of players is followed correctly.

c) carefully checks the numbers of substitutes to determine that they may legally enter the game before recording the information on the scoresheet.

d) records time-outs and notifies the second referee and the first referee the number of time-outs which have been charged to each team.

Article 3. DURING DECIDING GAME OF MATCH — During the deciding game of a match the scorer signals the referees when one of the teams has scored an eighth point and indicates that the teams should change playing areas.

Article 4. VERIFICATION OF FINAL SCORE — At the conclusion of a match, the scorer secures the signatures of the referees to verify that the winning score has been recorded and the match is official.

COMMENTARY ON RULE 16
THE SCORER

1) *GIVING INFORMATION TO TEAMS* — The scorer, when requested to do so by one of the referees, must tell either of the coaches or captains the number of substitutions and time-outs that have been charged to their team. Information pertaining to opponents will not be given to a coach or captain by the scorer.

2) *LINEUPS* — Prior to the start of each game of a match, the coach or team captain must send a lineup to the scorer on the official form provided. Opponents will not be permitted to see the lineup submitted by the opposing team prior to the start of play.

3) *RECORDING OF REMARKS* — The scorer must write all remarks pertaining to penalties, protests, etc., that occur during the progress of the game. Incidents leading to the disqualification of a player must be entered on the scoresheet.

4) *ORDER OF SERVICE* — The scorer must control the order of service. If a wrong server is in the service position at the time the referee whistles for service, the scorer shall wait until the ball is contacted during service and then sound a horn/ whistle and notify the referees of the fault.

5) *THE SCORE* — The scorer must score each point made by a team. The scorer must make sure that the score on the visible scoreboard agrees with the score recorded on the scoresheet. In the event of a discrepancy, the scoresheet shall be official and the discrepancy is not grounds for protest by a team.

RULE 17. THE LINE JUDGES

Article 1. POSITION DURING MATCH — During the match, the line judges will be stationed:

a) with two line judges, they must be placed diagonally opposite each other, one at each end of the court at the corner away from the serving area, at a minimum distance from the corner of 1 m. indoors and 3 m. outdoors.

b) With four line judges, one line judge shall be placed opposite each service area with the sideline extended approximately 2 m. behind the end line. One line judge shall be placed approximately 2 m. outside the sideline nearest the service area in line with the end line extended. Each line judge watches the line to which assigned.

Article 2. USE OF SIGNAL FLAGS — Each line judge shall be responsible for signaling to the first referee when a ball is "OUT" by raising the flag above the head, and when a ball is "IN" by pointing the flag towards the floor (ground) of the playing area.

Article 3. WHEN FLAGS NOT AVAILABLE — When flags are not available for use by line judges, they shall be instructed to raise the hands over the shoulders with the palms facing down to indicate when a ball is "OUT", and to extend the arms downward towards the playing area to indicate when a ball is "IN".

Article 4. OTHER DUTIES — The line judges shall also signal the first referee when:

a) foot fault errors are made by a player when serving.

b) the ball touches an antenna (above or on the net).

c) the ball does not pass over the net completely between the antennas or their indefinite extension.

d) The ball which is "OUT" was contacted by a player before contacting the floor (ground) or object outside the playing area.

COMMENTARY ON RULE 17
THE LINE JUDGES

1) *POSITION DURING MATCH* — *During the match, the line judges shall be standing in their assigned areas and shall move from those areas only for the purpose of avoiding interfering with players playing the ball or to better observe a ball crossing the net near an antenna.*

2) *NUMBER OF LINE JUDGES* — *For important competitions, it is recommended that four line judges be used.*

3) *SIGNALING THE FIRST REFEREE* — *Whenever a line judge needs to at-.t the attention of the first referee due to a fault committed by a player, or to a rude remark made by a player, the flag shall be raised above the head and waved from side to side.*

GAME PROCEDURES

These are the recommended standard procedures to be followed for the conduct of all official USVBA competition:

1. **OFFICIALS**
   a) The officials should be certified referees and scorers of the United States Volleyball Association.
2. **UNIFORMS**
   a) All players must wear uniforms prescribed by USBVA rule 5.
3. **PRE-GAME PROCEDURES**
   a) Well ahead of the starting time for the first game of the match, the first referee will call the captains together to conduct a coin toss.
   b) After the coin toss, the first referee will supervise warm-up periods with the serving team having use of the court for the first three minute warm-up period if the captains have elected to use separate warm-ups. If the team captains elect to warm-up together on the court, the first referee shall allow six minutes.
   c) At the end of the warm-up period, the first or second referee will walk to the center of the court and blow a whistle to indicate that the warm-up period is over and that players are to clear the court.
   d) Referees and other officials take their places.
   e) Teams line up on the end line of their respective areas. When both teams are ready and facing each other, the first referee will blow a whistle and motion for teams to take their positions on the court.
   f) Second referee will verify that players are on the court in positions listed on the official lineup sheets submitted to the scorer by each team. No corrections may be made unless there has been an error or omission made by the scorer or unless a legal substitution has been made prior to the start of play under the provisions of Rule 5, Commentary 7b. No other changes may be made in the lineups to correct an error made by teams in preparing the lineup sheets.
4. **START OF GAME**
   a) As soon as lineups are verified and teams are ready, the whistle is blown and a visual signal is given by the first referee for service to begin.
   b) Prior to the serve, the offensive players will halt their movements to allow officials to determine their positions. Continual movement may be misconstrued as screening.
5. **SUBSTITUTION PROCEDURES**
   a) Substitutes should approach the second referee in the substitution zone and wait to be recognized for entry. Substitutes entering the court and players leaving the court shall touch hands in the substitution zone and wait to be authorized to enter by the second referee.
6. **END OF GAME AND START OF NEXT GAME**
   a) Following the blowing of a whistle indicating the end of a game, players should line up on the end line of their playing areas. When both teams are in position and the second referee has verified that the winning point has been recorded, the first referee will blow a whistle and dismiss the teams for the rest period between games. Players may then leave the court.
   b) At the end of the rest period, the second referee will blow a whistle and teams shall immediately report to the end of their playing areas for the next game.
7. **CHANGE OF PLAYING AREAS DURING GAME**
   a) When teams are required to change playing areas during a deciding game of a

match, the first referee will blow a whistle and indicate both teams to move to the end line of their respective playing areas.
   b) After both teams are in position, the first referee will blow a whistle and motion for both teams to proceed in a counter-clockwise direction to the opposite end without delay.
   c) Substitutes and other team personnel will change benches so as to be seated on the side of their playing area.
   d) When teams are in position on the end line of the new playing areas, the first referee will blow a whistle and motion for both teams to move onto the court.
   e) The second referee will then verify that players are in their correct positions on the court.

8. **AT THE END OF THE MATCH**
   a) Following the blowing of whistle indicating the end of match, players will line up on the end line of their respective playing areas.
   b) When both teams are in position and the second referee has verified that the winning point has been recorded by the scorer, the first referee will signal with whistle and motion for the teams to form a single line and proceed to the center of the court to shake hands with the opponents.
   c) Referees will then proceed to the score table to verify and sign the scoresheets.
   d) The second referee will assure that the game ball is returned to the designated area for safekeeping.

COMMENTARY ON GAME PROCEDURES

(1) Unless a protest has been lodged in accordance with Rule 13, Article 3, referees are not to review the scoresheets at the conclusion of a match to determine if scorer errors have been made during the progress of the match. The first referee will determine that a winning score has been attained in each game and will record the final score in circles in the scoring column of each team. The first referee will then verify that the games are official by signing the bottom of each sheet.

UNITED STATES ONLY

SPECIAL RULES

The following four items have to do with competition other than regular six player team play. They are practically verbatim from previous years and it is acknowledged that there are probably more deviations than compliances in actual usage. The Committee on Rule and Interpretations solicits the experience of those groups and organization which do conduct and sponsor special competitions such as beach play, doubles, triples, co-ed, mixed doubles, etc.

   1) Co-Ed Play—The rules in general shall govern play for females and males on the same team with the following exceptions:

a) The serving order and positions on the court service shall be an alternation of male and female, or vice-versa.

b) When the ball is played more than once by a team, at least one of the contacts shall be made by a female player. Contact of the ball during blocking shall not constitute playing the ball. There is no requirement for a male player to contact the ball, regardless of the number of contacts by a team.

c) Uniforms of players shall be identical within the following provisions:
   (1) All female players shall be attired in identical jerseys and shorts.
   (2) All male players shall be attired in identical jerseys and shorts.
   (3) All uniforms shall be numbered in compliance with Rule 5, Article 1b. There shall be no duplicate numbers regardless of color of the jerseys.

d) When only one male player is in the front line at service, one male back line player may be forward of the attack line for the purpose of blocking.
   (1) Male back line players shall be governed by the provisions of Rule 8, Article 13 when playing the ball in other than blocking action.
   (2) Only one male back line player may be forward of the attack line when a male back line player is participating in a block.
   (3) No female back line player may participate in a block.

e) The height of the net for Co-Ed play shall be 2.43 m.

2) Reverse Co-Ed Play—The rules in general shall govern play for females and males on the same team with the following exceptions:

a) The serving order and positions on the court at service shall be an alternation of male and female, or vice-versa.

b) When the ball is played more than once by a team, at least one of the contacts shall be made by a male player. Contact of the ball during blocking shall not constitute playing the ball.

c) Uniforms of players shall be identical within the following provisions:
   (1) All female players shall be attired in identical jerseys and shorts.
   (2) All male players shall be attired in identical jerseys and shorts.
   (3) All uniforms shall be numbered in compliance with Rule 5, Article 1b. There shall be no duplicate numbers, regardless of color of the jerseys.

d) When only one female player is in the front line at service, one female back line player may be forward of the attack line for the purpose of blocking.
   (1) Female back line players shall be governed by the provisions of Rule 8, Article 13 when playing the ball in other than blocking action.
   (2) Only one female back line player may be forward of the attack line when a female back line player is participating in a block.

e) No male player may participate in a block.

f) No male player forward of the attack line may contact the ball and cause it to enter the opponent's playing area.

g) The height of net for Reverse Co-Ed play shall be 2.24 m.

3) BEACH PLAY—The rules in general shall govern play on beaches with the following exceptions:

a) The net height shall be 2.39 m. on hard packed sand and 2.36 m. on loose packed sand.

b) Playing areas shall be changed during each game after multiples of 5 points have been scored.

c) Ropes shall be used as boundary lines and center line.

4) DOUBLES PLAY—The rules in general shall govern for two-player (doubles) teams with the following exceptions:

   a) Each team area shall be 7.62 m. long.

   b) There shall be only two players with no substitutes on each team.

   c) There shall be only 2 positions, left and right half areas.

   d) The service shall be made from any position behind the end line.

   e) A game is won at 11 points, or if time is a factor, after 5 minutes of ball-in-play time has elapsed, whichever occurs first.

COMMENTARY ON SPECIAL RULES

1) *During co-ed play, if a team contacts the ball more than one time during offensive action, one of the contacts must be by a female player, but there is no restriction that prevents all three team hits being made by female players. Contact of the ball during blocking action does not count as one of the three team hits. Therefore, after a block, a male player may play the ball back over the net since such contact would be considered to be the first team hit.*

2) *During co-ed play, if the ball (other than a spiked ball) is contacted more than one time by a team and is directed over the net without being contacted by a female player, the hit does not become an illegal hit unless the ball passes fully beyond the vertical plane of the net (or is legally blocked).*

3) *During co-ed play, when there are two females and one male player in the front line at the time of service, one male backline player may be forward of the attack line for the purpose of participating in blocking action, but is restricted by the provisions of Rule 8 when playing the ball during offensive action.*

4) *During co-ed play, when there is one male back line player participating in a block, the other male back-line player shall remain behind the attack line until the ball has been contacted by the blockers or has been hit in such a manner that no block is possible.*

5) *During reverse co-ed play, if a team contacts the ball more than one time during offensive action, one of the contacts must be by a male player.*

6) *A male player taking off from on or in front of the attack line during reverse co-ed play may not hit the ball in such a manner that it enters the opponent's playing area. If such a hit is legally blocked across the plane of the net by an opponent, the ball is deemed to have crossed the plane of the net and the hit is illegal. If the ball is hit in such a manner that it would cross the net, but is contacted by a female player before crossing the net, the hit is legal.*

7) *There is no restriction on a male player hitting the ball into the opponent's court if the player takes off clearly behind the attack line before contacting the ball.*

8) *During reverse co-ed play, when there are two male and one female player in the front line at the time of service, one female player from the back line may be forward of the attack line for the purpose of participating in blocking action, but is restricted by the provisions of Rule 8 when playing the ball during offensive action.*

9) *During reverse co-ed play, when there is one female backline player participating in a block, the other female backline player shall remain behind the attack line until the ball has been contacted by the blockers or has been hit in such a manner that no block is possible.*

SIGNAL FOR ILLEGAL CONTACT

ILLEGAL CONTACT	A	CO-ED: No hit by a female player REVERSE COED: No hit by a male player

INTERPRETATIONS

Questions regarding interpretations of the present rules and current practices may be addressed to the Chairman of the Committee on Rules and Interpretations or to the Official Interpreter. Enclose a self addressed, stamped envelope with your inquiry for prompt return. All inquiries will receive replies. Because of the transition to international rules, some queries may involve consultations, but answers will be forwarded as promptly as possible.

CHANGES

Suggestions for changes, results of experiences, innovation proposals, and other rules related ideas may be transmitted through committee members, regional officials' chairmen or commissioners during the season. Explanation and rationale of proposed modifications must be in the chairman's hands before April 1, 1983, if they are to be considered at the annual meeting of the USVBA.

4

Illustrated Rules

The following illustrations of the rules are presented to supplement the rules and to clarify any question an official might have. It is hoped that they will provide a method to ease the transition from the printed word of the rule book to the visual experience of the game.

***Rule 4 Article 3.* During the game a player may not address the referee or umpire. Only the playing team captain may address the referee and shall be the spokesman for the players.**

***Court decorum:* Game officials should be treated with courtesy and respect.**

Rule 4 Article 6c. Committing an action which is intended to influence the decisions of officials is subject to penalty.

Rule 4 Article 6f. It is unsportsmanlike conduct and subject to penalty to distract an opponent who is in the act of playing the ball.

Rule 7 Article 8. After the ball is hit for the serve, players may move from their respective positions.

Rule 7 Article 8. At the time the ball is served, no back line player may be as near the net as the corresponding front line player.

"QUICK SERVE"

Rule 7 Article 1e. If the player serves before the referee's whistle, the service is cancelled and a reserve will be directed.

SERVER'S FOOT ILLEGAL

Rule 7 Article 1c. At the instant the ball is hit for service, no part of the server shall be in contact with the end line, the court or the ground floor outside the two lines marking the service area.

Rule 7 Article 2a. The referee will signal side-out and direct a change of service to the other team when the served ball touches the net.

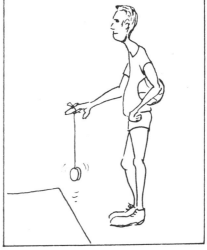

Rule 6 Article 9. Any act which, in the opinion of the referee, delays the game will be penalized.

Rule 7 Article 7. At the moment of service, it is illegal for players of the serving team to wave their arms, jump or form groups of two or more players for the purpose of forming a screen to conceal the action of the server.

Rule 7 Article 6. The team which receives the ball for service (following a side-out) shall rotate one position clockwise before serving.

Rule 8 Article 1. Each team is allowed a maximum of three successive contacts of the ball in order to return the ball to the opponent's area.

Rule 8 Article 3. The ball may be hit with any part of the body above and including the waist.

Rule 8 Article 6. When the ball comes to rest momentarily in the hands or arms of a player it is considered as being held.

Rule 8 Article 11e. Back line players may not block but may play the ball in any other position near or away from the block.

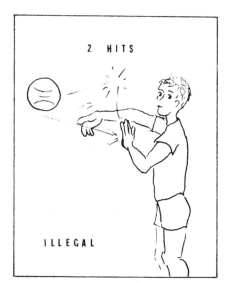

Rule 8 Article 5. A player contacting the ball more than once with whatever part of the body, without any other player having touched it between contacts, will be considered as having committed a double hit.

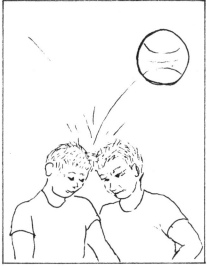

Rule 8 Article 8. When two players of the same team contact the ball simultaneously, this is considered as two contacts, and neither of the players may make the next play on the ball.

Rule 12 Article 12. When the ball, after having touched the top of the net and the opponent's block, returns to the attacker's side, this team then has the right of three more contacts in order to return the ball to the opponent's area.

Rule 9 Article 3. If the ball is driven into the net with such force as to cause the net to contact a member of the opposing team, such contact shall not be considered a fault on the part of the latter.

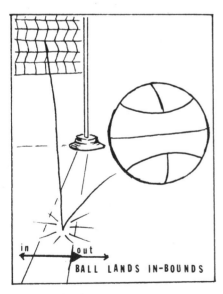

If any part of the ball lands on any boundary line, it is considered good (in-bounds).

Rule 8 Article 9. A hand or hands passing over the net after a spike is not a fault.

Rule 11 Article 4i. Contacting the ball over the net above the opponen't playing area before the opponent's action to send the ball toward the opposite side is made, shall constitute a fault.

Rule 11 Article 4p. Crossing the vertical plane of the net with any part of the body, with the purpose of interference or distraction of the opponent, while the ball is in play, constitutes a fault.

Rule 11 Article 4e. A point or side-out is declared (depending upon whether or not the serving or the receiving team committed the violation) when a player touches the ball twice consecutively.

Rule 11 Article 4g. A point or side-out is declared (depending upon whether or not the serving or the receiving team committed the violation) when a player touches the net or the antenna.

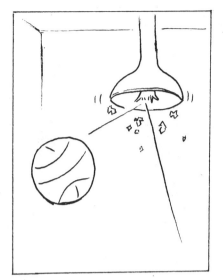

Rule 11 Article 4x. A side-out is declared against the serving team if it commits the fault or a point is awarded to the serving team if the other team is the offender, when a ball lands outside the court or touches an object outside the court.

Rule 11 Article 1. If during play, players from opposing teams commit simultaneous faults, a double fault shall be declared and a play-over will be directed.

Rule 14 Article 1. The referee is in full control of the match and the decisions of the referee are final.

Rule 15 Article 2d. The umpire should assist the referee by calling time if a foreign object enters the court.

Rule 5 Article 1a. It is forbidden to wear head gear or any article which could cause injuries during a game.

Rule 4 Article 2. Coaches, managers and captains are responsible for discipline and proper conduct of their team personnel.

Rule 1 Article 8. At game time, the minimum temperature shall not be below 10 degrees Centigrade (50 degrees Farenheit) at the playing area.

Co-ed Play: Special Rules. When the ball is played more than once by a team, at least one of the contacts shall be made by a female player.

5

Official's Signals

NOTE: In the continuing effort to standardize rules, protocol and other items pertaining to volleyball nationwide, the following list of play situations has been developed and the signals for each situation ruled on by the National Rules Interpreter:

Official Hand Signals

Official's Signals

4	**BALL OUT**	RAISE THE FOREARMS IN A VERTICAL POSITION, HANDS OPEN, PALMS FACING UPWARD	9	**FOUR HITS**	RAISE FOUR FINGERS
10	**CROSSING CENTER LINE**	POINT TO THE CENTER LINE AND AT THE SAME TIME INDICATE WITH THE SERVICE SIGNAL TO THE OPPONENTS SIDE. POINT TO THE PLAYER WHO COMMITTED THE FAULT	19	**BALL IN THE NET AT TIME OF SERVICE / PLAYER TOUCHING NET**	TOUCH THE NET WITH THE HAND. TOUCH THE NET WITH THE HAND AND POINT TO THE PLAYER WHO COMMITTED THE FAULT
11	**HELD BALL**	SLOWLY LIFT ONE HAND WITH THE PALM FACING UPWARD	20	**DOUBLE FOUL OR PLAY OVER**	RAISE THE THUMBS OF BOTH HANDS
12	**DOUBLE HIT**	LIFT TWO FINGERS IN VERTICAL POSITION	21	**BACK LINE BLOCK**	RAISE BOTH ARMS AND POINT TO THE PLAYER COMMITTING THE FAULT
13	**BALL CONTACTED BELOW THE WAIST**	POINT TO THE PLAYER WHO COMMITTED THE FAULT WITH ONE HAND AND MOTION WITH THE OTHER HAND FROM WAIST DOWNWARD	22	**OUT OF POSITION**	MAKE A CIRCULAR MOTION WITH THE HAND AND INDICATE THE PLAYER OR PLAYERS WHO HAVE COMMITTED THE FAULT
14	**END OF GAME OR MATCH**	CROSS THE FOREARMS IN FRONT OF THE CHEST	23	**OVER THE NET**	PASS THE HAND OVER THE NET AND POINT TO THE PLAYER WHO COMMITTED THE FAULT
15	**TIME OUT**	PLACE THE PALM OF ONE HAND HORIZONTALLY OVER THE OTHER HAND HELD IN VERTICAL POSITION FORMING THE LETTER T. FOLLOW BY POINTING TO THE TEAM REQUESTING THE TIME OUT	24	**BACK LINE SPIKER**	MAKE A DOWNWARD MOTION WITH THE FOREARM AND POINT TO THE PLAYER WHO COMMITTED THE FAULT
16	**SUBSTITUTION**	MAKE A CIRCULAR MOTION OF THE HANDS AROUND EACH OTHER	25	**BALL TOUCHING OBJECT**	POINT TO THE PLAYER OR TO THE OBJECT TOUCHED BY THE BALL
17	**BALL NOT RELEASED AT TIME OF SERVICE**	LIFT THE EXTENDED ARM, THE PALM OF THE HAND FACING UPWARD	26	**WARNING-PENALTY-EXCLUSION**	SHOW A YELLOW COLORED CARD. SHOW A RED COLORED CARD. SHOW BOTH THE YELLOW AND RED CARDS. CALL THE CAPTAIN OF THE OFFENDING TEAM AND ADVISE THE CAPTAIN WHETHER THE EXCLUSION IS FOR ONE OR MORE GAMES OR FOR THE ENTIRE MATCH
18	**DELAY OF SERVICE**	RAISE FIVE FINGERS IN A VERTICAL POSITION	27	**POINT**	RAISE THE INDEX FINGER AND ARM ON THE SIDE OF THE TEAM THAT SCORES THE POINT

*Signals used by permission of Alex Valow.